# HOW TO ATTEND THE EXTRAORDINARY FORM

**Dr Joseph Shaw**

All booklets are published
thanks to the generosity of the supporters
of the Catholic Truth Society

Nor should we see the newness of this mission as entailing a kind of displacement or forgetfulness of the living history which surrounds us and carries us forward.

Pope Francis, Post-Synodal Exhortation
*Evangelii Gaudium* (2013) 13

*ISBN 978 1 78469 631 3*

# Contents

# Introduction

Perhaps you've been to a celebration of the older form of the Catholic liturgy, usually called the 'Traditional Mass' or the 'Extraordinary Form', because it was a convenient time on a Sunday, as a one-off. Perhaps someone brought you to see it, or you were curious about it yourself. Perhps you came into a church where it was being celebrated, quite by chance. Perhaps you've never attended it, but have heard about it.

For Catholics used to a newer form of the Mass, the 'Ordinary Form', experiencing the older one raises a lot of questions. Why has the priest got his back to me? Why is everything in Latin? Is this kind of Mass even allowed? Most urgently: how am I supposed to participate in this liturgy? How can this be spiritually fruitful for me?

This booklet has been written to answer these questions, or as many of them as possible. It will be a brief answer; those who wish to read more are directed to the 'Further Reading' section at the end.

This booklet has been written by a layman, from the perspective of the laity. Like nearly all cradle Catholics in the Western Church today, I was brought up with the Ordinary Form Mass, celebrated in my mother tongue, and I didn't discover the Extraordinary Form until my late twenties. It is the astonishment felt at that moment of discovery, whether one views it positively, or with concern, or just with confusion, that this booklet is designed to address.

The Extraordinary Form of the Mass is the 'classical', the central and historically most widespread, form of Mass in the Western Church. For centuries it was attended by kings, soldiers, merchants, peasants, and children. It formed saints and scholars, converted sinners, sustained monks and nuns, inspired martyrs, and comforted the afflicted, in a complete range of social and economic conditions: from the basilicas of ancient Rome to the battlefields of the Second World War; from the mission stations of Africa, to the suffering Church in Communist China. Nothing should stop you engaging fruitfully with it, as they did.

## A note on terminology

When the Mass was reformed after the Second Vatican Council, the reformed Mass was called the *Novus Ordo Missae*, the 'New Order of Mass', or the *Missa Normativa*, the 'Normative Mass'. It became common to refer to the reformed Mass as the '*Novus Ordo*' or 'New Mass'; by parallel the previous form of Mass is sometimes called the '*Vetus Ordo*' or 'Old Mass'. Because the reformed Mass was generally celebrated in the language of the place where it was celebrated, the previous one was also called 'the

Latin Mass', or 'the Traditional Latin Mass'. It has also been called simply 'the Traditional Mass', the 'Tridentine Mass' (after the Council of Trent) or the 'Gregorian Mass' (after Pope Gregory the Great).

In 2007, Pope Benedict XVI ruled, in a document called *Summorum Pontificum*, that the older and newer forms of Mass should be regarded as two 'forms' or 'usages' of the Roman Rite: the 'Ordinary Form' of the Rite, and the 'Extraordinary Form' or 'Older Use' ('*Usus Antiquior*') of the Rite. (The legal significance of this distinction will be considered below.)

For the sake of clarity, this booklet uses the term 'Extraordinary Form', or 'EF', contrasting with the 'Ordinary Form' or 'OF', even when discussing the period before 2007.

# 1: How do I participate in the Extraordinary Form of the Mass?

## A glimpse of heaven

This booklet starts at the end: not with the history of the Mass, the Extraordinary Form's current legal status in the Church, or the symbolic significance of its individual ceremonies, but with how to participate in it. The question of participation arises from the experience of the Mass, an experience which is somewhat different from the experience of the Ordinary Form.

It may be a busy church or an empty one, and it may be a Low Mass or a Sung Mass (terms which will be explained below), but the impression created by the Extraordinary Form for a worshipper used to the Ordinary Form is distinctive. The Mass is taking place in the sanctuary: the priest bows before the altar, engages in a dialogue with the server, and proceeds to perform a series of prayers and ceremonies at the altar. There may be singing going on, but it is not led by the priest, and he doesn't in general appear to take any notice of it, but continues with the Mass while it continues. Members of the congregation may take part in some of the singing, and may make some responses, but except when he preaches, the priest does not even look at them. Many of the ceremonies are partially hidden from view, since the priest is facing away from the nave. Some of the words are said so quietly that even the server kneeling next to the celebrant can hardly hear them. The ones said aloud are in Latin.

Mass seems to be happening *over there*, in some place set apart from the congregation, and without the congregation's visible involvement. How to understand and engage with it is the central practical question for those new to attending the Extraordinary Form.

If you feel that you are being excluded, in a certain sense you are correct. We in the nave of the church are on the outside of something, but all the same we are looking in. We are, in fact, catching a glimpse of the heavenly liturgy. As the scholar Fr Michel Sinoir writes, noting the parallel with the liturgy of the Eastern Churches:

> The [Eastern] iconostasis symbolically is heaven, and its liturgy, which anticipates heaven, is celebrated only by members of the clergy. The nave is symbolically the earth, the abode of men and women who are preparing themselves to enter into glory. This is by analogy the same mystery as that of Christ-the-Bridegroom, renewing in the sanctuary his sacrifice, which is gratefully received by the Church-his-Bride who is still in pilgrimage here below.[1]

In this way, attending the Extraordinary Form can be understood as the privilege of seeing, from a distance, something of great solemnity and holiness. The things which contribute to the distance between the priest and his doings, and the congregation, are essential to creating the corresponding sense of the sacred. The fact that we can't see things clearly because the priest has his back to us, the use of Latin, silent prayers, the exclusion of the laity from the sanctuary except for vested servers: all these things serve to remind us that we are looking in at something very special, from the outside.

The distance here is not a distance of *understanding*. We can, if we wish, learn all about the ceremonies and prayers; those who learn to serve Mass must do so. We can follow all the texts in a hand missal. Even without doing either of those things, a Catholic attending Mass can, should, and usually does know what is going on, in general terms – it is the Sacrifice of the Mass – and in specific terms – the significance of each part of the Mass.

There is a distance all the same. It is the distance between heaven and earth, between what is holy and set apart, and what is profane, the everyday world: not between the good and the bad, but between the supernatural and the natural. By acknowledging the reality of the distance between heavenly and earthly things, the Extraordinary Form allows us to witness, to experience, heavenly things, and not only to experience them, but also to unite ourselves with them. In other words, by representing, symbolically and dramatically, the chasm which separates us mortals from the things of God, the EF makes it possible to bridge that chasm.

To repeat, the EF marks off the holiness of holy things: they are separated from us, and from all ordinary things. The sanctuary is separated from the nave; the language used is separate from the language of everyday speech; the type of music is a distinct, sacred style; the vestments of the priest are equally special, separate, and sacred. The point of all this is not to keep us away, however, but to draw us in. We can see and hear this special zone, and we unite ourselves to it by our prayer, because we unite our intentions and our prayers to those of the priest celebrating the Mass.

This is spiritual participation in the Mass. By uniting ourselves with something which is palpably holy, it is able to enter *us*, to transform us, as happens in a special way when we receive Holy Communion.

The Catholic religion contains something astonishing and awe inspiring: the real and living presence of Christ in the Blessed Sacrament on the altar, and the sacrifice Christ made of himself on Mount Calvary, offered in an unbloody manner in the Mass. Somehow the liturgy of the Mass must impress on the people both that this is what the Faith tells us it is, and also that we are invited to take part in these things. It is not so much a balance which needs to be struck, as a paradox which needs to be emphasised. Yes, it is a fearful thing to be in the presence of God. And yes, we may remain there, sinners as we are, and take part in the Church's own worship of God, which, because it is Christ's prayer and offering, is a perfect worship, acceptable to God. The Extraordinary Form does this precisely by *not* downplaying the holiness and otherness of what is taking place, and of what is present, but by making these qualities, in a certain way, visible. It is the holy nature of these things which we are invited first to acknowledge, and then to partake in.

Pope Francis expressed it, in addressing a Russian journalist about the liturgy of the Eastern Churches, in this way:

> In the Orthodox Churches, they have retained that pristine liturgy, which is so beautiful. We have lost some of the sense of adoration. The Orthodox preserved it; they praise God, they adore God, they sing, time does not matter. God is at the centre, and I would like to say, as you ask me this question, that this is a richness.[2]

Here Pope Francis himself makes the parallel between the Eastern Liturgy and the Western liturgy before the Second Vatican Council, which, for most Western Catholics, has been 'lost'. This loss is not absolute, however. It can still be experienced, as the Extraordinary Form.

## Practical advice

To participate in Mass means something specific: to unite
our prayers with those of the priest, and to offer ourselves
to God, together with the offering of Christ by the priest.
Some of the prayers of the Mass refer to this: for example,
when the priest speaks of the offering of 'my sacrifice and
yours', two distinct offerings are referred to.

Again, our attendance at Mass is an opportunity to bring
to God any specific intentions we may have, whether they
be our own needs, those of others, or loved ones who have
died. Mass is offered for 'the living and the dead'.[3]

Nevertheless, the exact way we participate prayerfully
in Mass is left open to us, and in the Extraordinary Form
the laity are given considerable freedom. Prayer, the
Church teaches us, is the lifting up of the mind and heart
to God,[4] and this can be done in many ways. We can do it
by following the prayers of the Mass in a hand missal; we
can say other appropriate prayers, which may be found in
devotional books; we can say other formal prayers, such
as the Rosary; or we can simply contemplate the action
of the Mass in a recollected way: knowing what we are
witnessing, and uniting ourselves with it.

In 1964, the novelist Evelyn Waugh wrote:

'Participation' in the Mass does not mean hearing our
own voices. It means God hearing our voices. Only

he knows who is 'participating' at Mass. I believe, to compare small things with great, that I 'participate' in a work of art when I study it and love it silently. No need to shout.[5]

Earlier, Pope Pius XII, having mentioned methods of participation such as reading the prayers of the Mass in a hand missal, added:

> [T]he needs and inclinations of all are not the same, nor are they always constant in the same individual. Who, then, would say, on account of such a prejudice, that all these Christians cannot participate in the Mass nor share its fruits? On the contrary, they can adopt some other method which proves easier for certain people; for instance, they can lovingly meditate on the mysteries of Jesus Christ or perform other exercises of piety or recite prayers which, though they differ from the sacred rites, are still essentially in harmony with them.[6]

As Pope Pius indicated, those who attend the Extraordinary Form regularly will find that different methods of directing their participation appeal to them on different occasions, depending on their mood and circumstances.

Broadly speaking, the structure of the Mass is the same in the Extraordinary as in the Ordinary Form, but there are a number of differences which can be confusing. If you are going to attend regularly, it makes sense to look at a booklet of the 'Ordinary of the Mass' (the fixed prayers) to see what is going on at each stage. This can be done at Mass, or outside of Mass. You may want to learn more from liturgical commentaries, some of which are listed in the 'Further Reading' section. Hand Missals provide all the texts of the Mass, including the variable parts. Today, many of these resources are available as apps on smart phones.

Equally, however, no one should feel a slave to a missal: on occasion, a missal can even feel like a distraction from the Mass. For those new to the Mass, some may find it best simply to experience the liturgy, without the mediation of printed texts. Above all, allow the Mass to speak to you.

### Different kinds of Extraordinary Form Mass

It may be helpful to explain briefly the different kinds of Mass which exist in the Extraordinary Form.

The key distinction is based on the liturgical resources which are available for a particular Mass. A 'Low' Mass can be celebrated by a priest with one or two servers or at a pinch with no server. The ceremonies are necessarily more simple than other forms of Mass, although it might be better to say that the ceremonies are *compressed*, which gives them a certain heightened intensity.

Especially with a small congregation, and perhaps in a small chapel, it can be very quiet, low-key and intimate, as well as relatively short, which makes it very practical as a Mass to be said or attended before or after a day's work, or in a lunch break.

If singers are available, to sing both the chants of the day and the 'ordinary' chants (*Kyrie*, *Gloria*, *Sanctus*, *Agnus Dei*), then mass can be sung. In its fullest form, this is the *Missa Solemnis*, called the 'High' or 'Solemn' Mass: this requires the assistance of a deacon and a subdeacon in addition to the celebrating priest. It involves a number of very beautiful ceremonies which aren't seen at other forms of the Mass, such as the 'Pax' (kiss of peace), and the proclamation of the Gospel away from the altar, with candles and incense. Because of the need for extra clergy, this is relatively uncommon.

There is also an intermediate form, *Missa Cantata*, called the 'Sung' or (in America) 'High' Mass. This does not require a deacon or subdeacon, but it does need singers. It can be (and nearly always is) celebrated with incense, but if there aren't enough servers available it can be celebrated without incense and just one or two servers. The ceremonies are a compromise between those of Low Mass and those of Solemn Mass. Sung Masses like this tend to be celebrated on Sundays and important feasts wherever the Extraordinary Form is well-established.

The Mass for the Dead, used at funerals and the anniversaries of loved ones, has certain unique features. For example, the prayers said by the priest and servers at the beginning of the Mass are shorter, and there may be a ceremony of sprinkling of holy water at the end of Mass, not only if a body is present prior to a burial service, but also of an empty coffin or coffin-stand, representing those for whom the Mass is offered. It can be celebrated as a Low, Sung, or Solemn Mass.

The reverent and restrained qualities of the Extraordinary Form Requiem Mass, as it is called (the opening chant begins '*requiem aeternam*', 'eternal rest'), makes it specially suitable for Masses celebrated for the deceased. It includes, among many very beautiful chants, the *Dies Irae*, which must count as one of the most influential pieces of music of any age or genre.

The Requiem's musical texts can be sung to polyphonic settings composed by some of the greatest Catholic musicians of history, as well as to their ancient Chant settings. This distinction applies to all sung Masses, although polyphonic composers tended not to compose settings for the text of the day for Sunday and feast-day Masses, but only the ordinary chants, so Masses where polyphony is sung will usually also have Gregorian Chant as well.

Polyphonic musical settings require singers with different voices – most often four: soprano, alto, bass, and tenor – and exist for all periods of music, from the earliest polyphonic music of the Renaissance, to Classical and modern music. Gregorian Chant has also been composed over many centuries, when new feasts have been created, but the core repertoire dates from between the eighth and tenth centuries. Both can be heard on occasion in the

Ordinary Form, but at the Extraordinary Form they are heard more frequently, because the liturgical law does not allow them to be replaced by hymns in sung Masses.

## A note on posture during Mass

Those new to the Extraordinary Form may notice the people doing a bit more kneeling than in the Ordinary Form. A more fundamental difference, however, is that whereas rules are laid down for the people's postures in the OF, in the EF it is a matter of personal preference and local custom, and there is in practice a fair amount of variation between congregations.

All congregations stand for the Gospel and kneel for the Consecration. For the rest of Mass you can suit yourself, with due respect for local practice and what may inconvenience or distract others. The instructions given in handbooks (which themselves vary) should be regarded as suggestions, not hard-and-fast rules.

## The tone and ethos of the Extraordinary Form

It was noted above that the Extraordinary Form impresses us with a sense of the sacred. It is useful to note the means it uses – and does not use – to do this.

There is nothing bombastic about the Extraordinary Form. If we consider its texts, the traditional architecture and fittings of a church, traditional vestments, and above all, the form of sacred music specially developed to serve it – Gregorian Chant – there is nothing which judges us, bullies or harangues us, or seeks to overwhelm us with sentimentality.

Pope Pius X insisted on Gregorian Chant, and those forms of music most akin to it, as most appropriate to the liturgy,[7] and his words were echoed by the Second Vatican Council.[8] In the chant and in the texts and ceremonies of the Mass, the liturgy has a great emotional range, from penance and grief, to expectation and joy, but this is expressed with a great economy of means, and without emotional manipulation.

The predictability and steadiness of the ancient liturgy gives the more dramatic moments, for example during the ceremonies of Holy Week, special force, just as the silence of the central prayers of the Mass accords a greater impact to the ringing of the bell for the Consecration. The language of the prayers is restrained, and yet insistent.

Ceremonies, chants, and the use of silence as well as the spoken word, enable the liturgy to enter the worshipper not only at the intellectual level. As Pope John Paul II noted of the traditional liturgy of the Eastern Churches, which has much in common with that of the Western Church:

> The lengthy duration of the celebrations, the repeated invocations, everything expresses gradual identification with the mystery celebrated with one's whole person.[9]

The venerable age of the Extraordinary Form is another aspect of its ethos. It connects us today with the Catholics of every century, back to the times of the early Church, the Age of the Fathers. Popes, Doctors, and saints prayed the very same words and listened to the same readings, and many of the things they said about the Mass make sense in the context of the Extraordinary Form as celebrated today.[10] This unity, through time as well as space, gives a special sense of solidarity with our predecessors in the Faith when we participate in the EF.

The overall effect of the tone and ethos of the Extraordinary Form is that of *peace*. When we attend the Extraordinary Form we leave the noisy and busy world, and enter a timeless oasis of calm. In this way it gives great consolation to those attached to it, and it does not make demands upon us at odds with the feelings we may have: our stress, exhaustion, grief, or, for that matter, our joy. For many people, the EF is, in its own words (speaking of heaven), 'a place of refreshment, light, and peace': *locus refrigerii, lucis et pacis*.[11]

## 2: What does it mean?
## Ceremonies and prayers

In this chapter a number of specific issues about Mass celebrated in the Extraordinary Form will be addressed. They have been chosen principally because they are the issues which those new to this form of Mass most often find surprising, rather than because they are the most important aspects of the Mass.[12] What is most important of all in the Mass are things the Extraordinary Form has in common with Ordinary Form: the Sacrifice and the Sacrament. The following discussion will take for granted a degree of familiarity with Mass in itself, to address what is different about the EF.

### *Ad orientem*: Facing East

One of the most immediately striking features of the Extraordinary Form is the way the priest faces away from the people for nearly all of the Mass. The Ordinary Form can be celebrated like this, '*ad orientem*', but this is rare.

The practice is called *ad orientem* because the priest is facing the direction of the rising sun (from the Latin '*oriens*', for 'rising'). Until the sixteenth century, churches were usually built with the altar at their geographical east end, but even when this is not the case, we can talk about 'liturgical east': what is symbolically regarded as the east. In any case, in the practice of the Extraordinary Form, the priest faces the same direction as the people, towards the crucifix.

The psychological impact of this arrangement is considerable, because it makes it immediately clear that the priest is not addressing himself to the congregation, except for the moments in the Mass when he turns around specifically to do so. The dramatic distinction between these moments and the rest of the Mass underlines the reality that the Mass is an act of worship directed towards God, and not something directed towards the people. In this act of worship, the priest is united with the people, leading them in prayer: the priest is *with* the people, representing the people before God, rather than, as it were, coming from a different direction, and facing them.

Another effect of worship *ad orientem* is to minimise the significance of the priest as an individual. For much of the Mass we cannot see his face, and even when he does turn around the rubrics instruct him to keep his eyes lowered. There is therefore no eye-contact, no expression of the priest's personality, and no reliance on his personal charisma, to engage the congregation. In the absence of those things, we are reminded that the priest celebrates Mass not as himself, but *in persona Christi*: Christ acts through him so completely that he is able to say the words of Christ, at the Consecration, as if they were his own: 'This is my Body... This is the chalice of my Blood... Do this in memory of me.'

The importance of *ad orientem* celebration was particularly championed in the theological writings of Joseph Ratzinger, before his election as Pope Benedict XVI. He was concerned that worship '*versus populum*' (facing the people) could lead to a community becoming closed in on itself. As Pope, Benedict restored *ad orientem* worship in the Sistine Chapel. He wrote:

> Looking at the priest has no importance. What matters is looking together at the Lord. It is not now a question of dialogue, but of common worship, of setting off towards the One who is to come. What corresponds with the reality of what is happening is not the closed circle, but the common movement forward expressed in a common direction for prayer.[13]

The reference to 'the One who is to come' relates to the reason for the choice of east as the common direction. The east has come to represent the Second Coming of Christ, by reference to Matthew 24:27: 'For as lightning cometh out of the east, and appeareth even into the west: so shall the coming of the Son of man be.'[14] This means that a shared eastward direction of worship is given an eschatological dimension. Mass not only looks back to the crucifixion, but also forward to Christ's return in glory.

Although, as noted, celebration of the Ordinary Form *ad orientem* is rare, the issue was not addressed at the Second Vatican Council, and as illustrated by Joseph Ratzinger's writings (among many others), it remains a hotly debated liturgical issue. The practice of worship *ad orientem* is also used by the Eastern Churches, and the suggestion that they adopt the now usual western practice has been strongly resisted by the Congregation for the Eastern Churches:

> It is not a question, as is often claimed, of presiding the celebration with the back turned towards the people, but rather of guiding the people in pilgrimage towards the Kingdom, invoked in prayer until the return of the Lord.
>
> Such practice...is thus of profound value and should be safeguarded...[15]

We will return to some of the ongoing debates within the Ordinary Form in Chapter 8.

## Silence

Another immediately striking thing about the Extraordinary Form is the silence. Almost the whole of the Canon (the Eucharistic Prayer) and a number of other prayers are said by the priest so quietly that they cannot be heard. This is related to another contrast between the two Forms, which is that at Sung Masses singing by the choir continues over certain parts of the Mass in the Extraordinary Form, whereas in the Ordinary Form the priest's proclamation of the liturgical texts more often has to wait until any singing has finished.

The silence of the most important part of the Mass, including the words of Consecration, distinguishes it from what precedes and follows it, and marks it off as something particularly special. When Mass is sung, there is singing before and after, by the priest and by the choir (the Preface and the *Sanctus* before, and the *Pater Noster* and the *Agnus Dei* after). Singing is one way of giving a text greater prominence and solemnity. To go beyond this, to show that the solemnity of the Mass has risen to yet higher level, there is silence. It signals that we have arrived at a point where, for the congregation, words no longer suffice. For the priest, it is the point where he must commune, alone, with God, as when the High Priest of the Jewish Temple passed behind the curtain into the Holy of Holies: 'the Lord is in his holy temple. Let all the earth keep silence before him.'[16] And again, it recalls the silence of the crucifixion.

Those who have not experienced it may find it hard to imagine, but during the silence of the Canon of the Mass one can become oddly detached even from the noise of people digging up the road outside, or of small children in the congregation. It is not, after all, a silence indicating that nothing is happening, but a silence of intense and deep activity. As Joseph Ratzinger, to quote him again, expressed it:

> Anyone who has experienced a church united in the silent praying of the Canon will know what a really *filled* silence is. It is at once a loud and penetrating cry to God and a Spirit-filled act of prayer. Here everyone does pray the Canon together, albeit in a bond with the special task of the priestly ministry. Here everyone is united, laid hold of by Christ, and led by the Holy Spirit into that common prayer to the Father which is the true sacrifice – the love that reconciles and unites God and the world.[17]

This silence powerfully stimulates the worshipper to contemplative prayer, and its value is heightened, rather than diminished, by the insistent noise of modern life. As Pope John Paul II wrote, on the role of silence in the liturgy: 'In a society that lives at an increasingly frenetic pace, often deafened by noise and confused by the ephemeral, it is vital to rediscover the value of silence.'[18]

We may say, indeed, that silence is God's language. As Pope Benedict XVI wrote:

> If God speaks to us even in silence, we in turn discover in silence the possibility of speaking with God and about God. We need that silence which becomes contemplation, which introduces us into God's silence and brings us to the point where the Word, the redeeming Word, is born.[19]

## Latin

In light of the role of silence in the Extraordinary Form, it is less surprising that the rest of the Mass is celebrated in a special language, Latin. If one need not even *hear* the most important part of the Mass, in order to participate with it with special intensity, then it follows that one need not understand, at a word-by-word level, other parts of the Mass, to participate in them.

As noted in Chapter 1, neither the inaudibility nor the use of Latin in practice create a barrier of understanding between the worshipper and the liturgy, since members of the congregation can consult a hand missal, printout, or smartphone, to see exactly what is being said, translated into a wide variety of languages. It does, on the other hand, mark off the liturgy as something special and distinct from ordinary life. When we enter into the Latin zone, so to speak, we are entering into a spiritual space.

In this way Latin powerfully reinforces the atmosphere created by the architecture and fittings of a church building, the special vestments worn by the clergy, the distinct type of music appropriate to the Mass, and so on. The 2011 English translation of the Mass followed guidelines set out in the Instruction *Liturgiam Authenticam*, which called for a 'sacred style that will come to be recognised as proper to liturgical language.'[20] The use of Latin takes this principle a step further. In the Western Church, the liturgical language *par excellence* is Latin.

Latin long ago ceased to be the cradle language of any particular community, a fact which strengthens its role as a universal, sacred, language for the many language-communities which make up the Western Church, a role increasingly useful for the multi-lingual parishes now found in many parts of the world, and for travellers.

The Latin of the Mass was never, in truth, the language of the street, or of the public speaker. Not only is it often flowery and poetic, but it is strongly marked by the influence of Greek and Hebrew, and makes extensive use of repetition and deliberate archaism. It was always intended to be what it is: a distinct, holy, language, to be used only in the liturgy.[21]

Pope Paul VI, who authorised Mass to be celebrated in vernacular languages, nevertheless remarked in 1966 that liturgical Latin was 'an abundant well-spring of Christian civilisation and a very rich treasure-trove of devotion.'[22] In 1969, he told a General Audience:

> The introduction of the vernacular will certainly be a great sacrifice for those who know the beauty, the power and the expressive sacrality of Latin. We are parting with the speech of the Christian centuries; we are becoming like profane intruders in the literary preserve of sacred utterance.

Again, he refers to 'that language of the angels', 'the divine Latin language'.[23]

It would seem that Pope Paul felt that his own appreciation of Latin was characteristic of an educational elite. It is certainly true that learning Latin and becoming familiar with the Latin of the Vulgate (the version of the Bible usually used in the Extraordinary Form) brings great rewards, in opening up the poetic qualities of the liturgy, and its frequent scriptural references. It has become evident, however, that the Latin liturgy is appreciated by many whose knowledge of Latin is limited or non-existent.

The explanation for this has already been indicated: as a marker of the sacred, it enables us to enter into the spirit of the liturgy more fully. As Pope John Paul II remarked:

> There are also those people who, having been educated on the basis of the old liturgy in Latin, experience the lack of this 'one language,' which in all the world was an expression of the unity of the Church and through its dignified character elicited a profound sense of the Eucharistic Mystery.[24]

One does not have to understand the Latin text word by word as it is spoken to perceive – and be moved by – the solemn character with which it clothes the liturgy. The meaning of the text can be immediately available to the worshipper in printed form, but the impression made by the *form* of the text, the fact that it is proclaimed in an ancient, sacred language, of unique grandeur and gravity, is also of considerable value.

This is something well understood by Christians in the Eastern Churches, most of whom use special sacred languages for the liturgy, whether it be an archaic form of Greek, Church Slavonic in Russia, or Ge'ez in Ethiopia. The same is true of many non-Christian religions: non-Arab-speaking Muslims pray in classical Arabic, and Hindus, Buddhists, and Jains in Sanskrit. It would, in fact, be a strange thing if Western Christianity had no sacred language of its own.

The repeated liturgical use of Latin does, in fact, establish a familiarity over time which enables the worshipper not only to recognise what part of the Mass is taking place (the *Gloria*, for example, or the *Agnus Dei*), but also to know the fixed prayers of the Mass well enough to understand them as they are proclaimed in Latin. As noted in Chapter 1, it makes sense to familiarise yourself with the Mass with a translation to hand. Soon, many key Latin words will become familiar.

Serious study of Latin is not necessary for a profound appreciation of the liturgy celebrated in Latin, but of course it is not to be discouraged. Pope John Paul II was addressing Catholics who probably never attended the liturgy in Latin when he quoted Cicero's remark: 'It is not so much a matter of distinction to know Latin as it is disgraceful not to know it.'[25]

## The Lectionary

The differences between the Lectionaries of the Ordinary and the Extraordinary Forms are not so striking to the ordinary Mass-goer as the issues just dealt with, but the topic is included because it is sometimes said, even by those sympathetic to the EF, that the older Lectionary is clearly deficient by comparison with the reformed one. The reason for this is that, with its multi-year cycle and additional reading on Sundays, it includes more Scripture. The rationale of the Lectionary in the Extraordinary Form accordingly demands some explanation.

At each Mass in the Extraordinary Form there is (with a few exceptions) just one non-Gospel reading, and a reading from the Gospel. There are readings assigned for each Sunday and important feast-day of the year, for every day of Lent, and for Votive Masses. Less important saints' days have readings (and other 'proper' texts, such as the Collect) from the 'Commons of the Saints', a few of which exist for each category of saint: Pope, Doctor, Martyr, Holy Woman, and so on. A regular worshipper at the Extraordinary Form will in time become familiar with the Sunday Gospels, and a weekday Mass-goer will even more quickly begin to recognise the readings given for many of the saints: the Confession of St Peter (Matthew 16:13-19) for the Popes; the description of the 'valiant woman' (Proverbs 31) for holy women; the story of the woman in the crowd praising the Blessed Virgin Mary (Luke 11:27-28), for many of her Votive Masses. These readings are often related to, and sometimes quoted in, the other texts of the day.

One consequence of this system is that the readings and prayers of each day's Mass always pertain to the feast of the day, instead of simply being the readings which come after the readings of the previous day. On Sundays, the readings form a series which relates to the season, working up to a climax of eschatological expectation, most notably, just before and at the beginning of Advent, and giving advice on penance before and during Lent. Without going into technical details, this kind of festal or seasonal pertinence is more difficult to achieve with the '*lectio continuo*' ('continuous reading') principle which governs the Lectionary of the Ordinary Form.

The appropriateness of the readings to the day – and the people's greater familiarity with a smaller set of readings – have something to be said for them: there is loss as well as gain with the larger set of readings provided in the OF. Curiously, the much larger reformed Lectionary also omits some of the passages used in the older Lectionary; this points to another aspect of the contrast between the Ordinary and Extraordinary Forms.

The omitted passages are generally those which were regarded, when the new Lectionary was being developed in the late 1960s, as in some sense 'difficult'. The prophet

Daniel's vision of the Abomination of Desolation in the Temple is not referred to in the readings of the Ordinary Form, either in the Gospels or in the Old Testament;[26] nor is Jesus' warning that his disciples would be ejected from the Synagogues,[27] or St Paul's admonition to the Corinthians to receive Holy Communion with a clear conscience:[28] examples could be multiplied. Similarly, the proper and the ordinary prayers of the Missal were carefully edited by the reformers to remove references and themes which they thought could be off-putting to modern people.

Thus in attending the Extraordinary Form one is far more often brought up short by aspects of Scripture and Tradition which otherwise receive less attention: the realities of persecution, the hostility of 'the world', our sinfulness and need for contrition and penance, divine punishment and God's grace. There is a certain brutal honesty about it: things are not being swept under the carpet. Whether one is sated with the unsatisfying sweetness of consumerism, or suffering under the harsher side of modern life, the astringent quality of the Extraordinary Form can serve as a useful corrective, and even a relief.

### Liturgical seasons and the calendar

The issue of liturgical seasons is included here mainly because it can be a source of confusion. Christmas and Easter obviously fall on the same days in the Ordinary and the Extraordinary Form, but there are also a number of differences.

The most important is the season of three Sundays preceding Lent, during which the celebrant wears violet (purple). This is a season of preparation for Lent, called 'Septuagesima', as it starts roughly seventy days before Easter.

Since Lent is itself a preparation for Easter, getting ready for Lent might seem redundant, but it does have its uses. A season of penance benefits from some preparation, no less than a season of celebration. Mgr (later, Archbishop) Annibale Bugnini, the Vatican official who was responsible for the abolition of Septuagesima, records an interesting defence of it by Pope Paul VI:

> On one occasion Pope Paul VI compared the complex made up of Septuagesima, Lent, Holy Week and Easter Triduum, to the bells calling people to Sunday Mass. The ringing of them an hour, a half-hour, fifteen and five minutes before the time of Mass has a psychological effect and prepares the Faithful materially and spiritually for the celebration of the liturgy. [29]

From a practical point of view, it can serve to remind us to decide in good time what form our Lenten penance should take: what to 'give up', or what extra devotions or good works to adopt.

In a somewhat similar way, the calendar of the Extraordinary Form has more days on which an important feast is prepared for, or celebrated. The season of Christmas is longer, lasting until the feast of the Presentation on 2nd February; Pentecost has an 'octave', being followed by a week of special Masses focused on the Holy Spirit's coming and what this means for us; a number of important feasts (Christmas Day, the Ascension, the Assumption and some others) have a 'vigil' with its own proper Mass, a day of spiritual preparation for the feast.

The liturgical scholar, Fr Pius Parsch, writing before the Second Vatican Council, gives a practical explanation of octaves, which applies *mutatis mutandis* to vigils:

> Mother Church is a good psychologist; she understands human nature perfectly. When a feast comes, the soul is amazed and not quite prepared to think profoundly upon its mystery; but on the following days the mind finds it easy to consider the mystery from all sides, sympathetically and deeply; and an eighth day affords a wonderful opportunity to make a synthesis of all points covered.[30]

Another feature of the Extraordinary Form calendar, which is only rarely found in the Ordinary Form, is the very ancient 'Ember Days'. These are four sets of three days (Wednesday, Friday, and Saturday), distributed through the year, as special liturgical days, with their own Masses. The Mass on the Saturday has five readings from the Old

Testament, in addition to the usual Epistle and Gospel, reminiscent of the Easter Vigil. They are reminders of our need for penance, petition and thanksgiving in each season, although the spring one coincides with the Octave of Pentecost, and the colour is red rather than violet.

Considered overall, the calendar of the Extraordinary Form gives us more contrasts: more days of violet vestments with references to fasting, more days of celebration, and also more minor saints' days. Many of these saints are of great antiquity, and are another way the EF reinforces our communion with the earliest Christian centuries.

On 'free' (ferial) days outside Lent, priests can choose to celebrate the Mass of the previous Sunday or a Votive Mass, an optional Mass for a particular devotion. The Missal recommends some for each day of the week. Mass-goers on ferial weekdays might get a Mass of the Blessed Sacrament, the Sacred Heart, St Joseph, Our Lady (on Saturdays), a Mass for the Dead or one of many others. These Votive Masses are a great boost to the devotion of the Faithful towards these and similar objects.

Every day of Lent, on other hand, has its own Mass, which can only be superseded by a feast of some importance.

One might say, as far as the calendar of the Extraordinary Form goes, that there is always something special going on.

## The reception of Communion

An issue of very practical relevance is the way Holy Communion is distributed in the Extraordinary Form: the Host is given to kneeling communicants (unless illness or disability makes kneeling impossible), and on the tongue, and the communicant does not say 'amen'. Furthermore, the Precious Blood is not given to the Faithful, but consumed only by the celebrant.

Not for the first time in this booklet, Pope Paul VI provides an eloquent defence of a practice which, under him, was almost to disappear. He (or to be exact, the Congregation for Divine Worship under him), wrote in 1969:

> In view of the state of the Church as a whole today, this manner of distributing Holy Communion [on the tongue] must be observed, not only because it rests upon a tradition of many centuries but especially because it is a sign of the reverence of the Faithful towards the Eucharist. The practice in no way detracts from the personal dignity of those who approach this great Sacrament and it is a part of the preparation needed for the most fruitful reception of the Lord's body.
>
> This reverence is a sign of Holy Communion not in 'common bread and drink' but in the Body and Blood of the Lord. …

In addition, this manner of communicating, which is now to be considered as prescribed by custom, gives more effective assurance that Holy Communion will be distributed with the appropriate reverence, decorum, and dignity; that any danger of profaning the Eucharistic species, in which 'the whole and entire Christ, God and man, is substantially contained and permanently present in a unique way,' will be avoided; and finally that the diligent care which the Church has always commended for the very fragments of the consecrated bread will be maintained: 'If you have allowed anything to be lost, consider this a lessening of your own members.' [31]

From the laity's point of view, there can be no doubt that reception on the tongue, together with kneeling, 'underscore the Real Presence with an exclamation point,'[32] as Pope Benedict XVI expressed it, when explaining his own decision to insist on this manner of reception in papal celebrations in St Peter's in Rome.

The rationale of placing the Host directly onto the communicant's tongue was explained, at the time of Pope Benedict's decision, by reference to a passage of St Thomas Aquinas:

Out of reverence towards this Sacrament, nothing touches it, but what is consecrated; hence the corporal and the chalice are consecrated, and likewise the priest's hands, for touching this Sacrament. Hence, it is not lawful for anyone else to touch it except from necessity.[33]

It is interesting to note that, although this manner of receiving the Host took time to develop in the West (and developed in a somewhat different way in the East), the well-known description given by St Cyril of Jerusalem of receiving the Host in the hand in his own day does not involve the communicant picking up the Host with his fingers.[34] Similarly, although in the early centuries communicants received the Precious Blood, this was accompanied by an attitude of great reverence towards the chalice, and communicants were not allowed to touch it, even with their lips.[35] It is the same attitude of concern for holy things, both the Sacred Species and the vessels, which lies behind the practice, of many centuries' duration, of the Extraordinary Form today.

## Head coverings

Something visible in many congregations attending Mass in the Extraordinary Form, but much more rarely in the Ordinary Form, is the custom of women covering their heads, usually with a lace mantilla (called in America a 'chapel veil').

This practice, which was an obligation of canon law under the 1917 Code of Canon Law (which was superseded by the 1983 Code), goes back to the primitive Church, together with the custom for men to uncover their heads. It has been rediscovered by many women whose interest in the Church's traditions has been piqued by their experience of the Extraordinary Form.

It is St Paul who insists, rather sharply, on this custom: 'If anyone is inclined to dispute this, we have no other practice, nor do the churches of God.'[36] So what is its precise significance?

It is commonly said that the early Church adopted it in deference to local cultural norms, and this explanation has even found its way into official documents.[37] However, the practice St Paul describes does not correspond to Greek, Roman, or Jewish habits. Greek men and women alike sacrificed to the gods with uncovered heads; Romans did so with covered heads; and for the Jews, the covering of the head for prayer, sacrifice, or in the presence of the divine, was associated with men, not women, as it is to this day.[38] To distinguish men and women, and have men take off their headcoverings, and women keep theirs on, seems if anything an inversion of Jewish practice, and has nothing to do with the practice of the pagans of St Paul's world.

We are forced, therefore, to take seriously the reasons St Paul himself gives for this practice, reasons which continue to have meaning for us today. St Paul connects his rationale for covering or uncovering the head in the liturgy with the analogy of Christ as the bridegroom of the Church, which he compares with the relationship between the head and the body. Christ is the head of the Church, and the Church's human members make up the mystical

Body of Christ. This is analogous, St Paul tells us, to the human family, in which the husband is the head, the wife (and other members of the family) the body. Christ loves the Church, and a husband should love his wife as his own body, and 'he is the saviour of his body'. In both cases this self-sacrificial love corresponds to leadership, and should be reciprocated with respect (Ephesians 5:22-24).

Head coverings come into this as a marker of subordination (1 Corinthians 11:10) and of holiness (1 Corinthians 12:23). It symbolises, therefore, the Church as the spotless bride, which the female members of the congregation represent. This idea was taken up by Pope John Paul II when he wrote of women having a 'spousal character':[39]

> This spousal dimension, which is part of all consecrated life, has a particular meaning for women, who find therein their feminine identity and as it were discover the special genius of their relationship with the Lord.[40]

Women more readily represent the Church as bride, and men Christ the bridegroom – a fact obviously linked to the teaching of the Church that only men can be ordained as priests.

The theologian Manfred Hauke notes, having referred to the Blessed Virgin Mary as 'archetype of "Mother Church"':[41]

> In an analogical way, therefore, women, too, are representative *and* embodiments of the Church. As

opposed to men and the male priesthood, they symbolise a reality with which they are themselves identical.

Men symbolise the authority of Christ, to which they are themselves subject.

To what extent St Paul's theology of the Church as Bride of Christ can or should be disentangled from his teaching about authority in the household goes beyond the scope of this booklet: I can only urge readers to follow up the references to St Paul's letters, and look up the way his words have been understood by the Fathers and Doctors of the Church.

What we can say is that for a woman to take up this custom, which goes back to the earliest days of the Church and is still maintained in the Eastern Churches, is to demonstrate the spousal character of the Church in relation to Christ, in a way which the male members of the congregation cannot so easily do. This spousal character, in relation to Christ, is a matter of fidelity and holiness, since the Church, for all her human shortcomings, will be presented as a chaste virgin to Christ at the end of time (2 Corinthians 11:2), because she has been saved by him.

Today, head coverings are not part of mainstream fashion, and for women to cover their heads in church, particularly with a special head-covering not used in any other context, is an example of a phenomenon noted by Pope John Paul II: 'the liturgy, though it must always be properly inculturated, must also be counter-cultural.'[42] The counter-cultural nature of the gesture gives it heightened power to witness to the holiness of the liturgy, as a place where different rules apply.

## Male altar servers

The issue of women covering their heads in church leads naturally to the issue of only men and boys being allowed to serve at Mass in the Extraordinary Form. They differ, however, in that while head-coverings are no longer an obligation deriving from the law of the Church, females are still excluded from serving in the Extraordinary Form by the law of the Church, as has been confirmed by the competent authorities in Rome. This is because the celebration of the Extraordinary Form is governed by the liturgical law contained in the 1962 *Missale Romanum*.[43]

Lay servers substitute for those formally given this task as acolytes, who can be men only, and are most often seminarians. This is true both under the old rules, when the role of acolyte was one of the 'minor orders', and under the new rules, when the role of acolyte is an 'instituted ministry'. In the Extraordinary Form, we can see that in Sung Mass with just one priest and lay servers, the servers perform many tasks allocated to the deacon and the subdeacon in Solemn (High) Mass.

Altar servers are related, then, to the priesthood, as a subordinate rung on a hierarchy reaching up to the priesthood, and as an intimate assistant of the priest in the celebration of Mass. The issue has special weight in the Extraordinary Form because the role of server at Mass is more complex and of greater importance, and while it is possible for a priest to celebrate Mass without a server, this is something which priests, and the Faithful attached to the Extraordinary Form, seek to avoid. It is not unknown, in fact, for one priest to serve another priest's Mass, where others servers are unavailable, and the ability to serve Mass is very widespread among men who regularly attend the Extraordinary Form. In short, it is taken very seriously.

Females were permitted to serve the Ordinary Form for 'specific local reasons' in 1994[44], a concession made in the context of the debate about the ordination of women. (The Church of England ordained its first female priests in 1992.) The context makes this concession understandable, but the witness given by the Extraordinary Form also retains its value. The restriction of the service of the altar to males gives dramatic expression to the appropriateness of the male priesthood: it says that even the priest's assistants, and indeed all those appearing in the sanctuary during Mass, must be males.

## Conclusion

A parallel point can be made about other aspects of the Extraordinary Form which have already been discussed. We might say, about the reception of Holy Communion kneeling and on the tongue, that this practice is by no means necessary for Catholics to believe in the Real Presence, and this is true, but as Pope Benedict has already been quoted as saying, it marks it with 'an exclamation point'. The wearing of head-covering by women at Mass is not a necessary underpinning for the Church's teaching on the complementarily of the sexes, but it certainly makes that teaching more visible. The celebration of Mass *ad orientem*, with a common direction of worship for priest and people, is not required for the teaching on the eschatological meaning of the Mass; nevertheless, as Christoph, Cardinal Schönborn remarked, in a retreat preached to Pope John Paul II:

> Yet how important such signs are for 'incarnating' the faith. The common prayer of priest and Faithful *ad orientem* connected this cosmic 'orientation' with faith in the Resurrection of Christ, the *sol Invictus* [unconquered sun], and with his *Parousia* in glory. [45]

In these ways, the Extraordinary Form makes the perennial teaching of the Church visible, audible, and dramatic, expressing it in memorable symbols.

This is why the ceremonies and prayers of the Extraordinary Form have value: because they express the beauty of the Faith. To mention some issues not already discussed, the priest's consistent acts of reverence towards the Blessed Sacrament on the altar; his repeated prayers for purification; the visible preparation for Mass with the 'Prayers at the Foot of the Altar'; the genuflection at the reference to the Incarnation in the Last Gospel: the realities which these things seek to express – the Real Presence, our sinfulness, the Incarnation – are things which we must hold with lively faith, for they are truths without which we cannot live in the Faith. To go beyond a merely intellectual assent to them, we need to meditate upon them, and let them enter into us. To quote again the words of Pope John Paul II, the liturgy can facilitate the 'gradual identification with the mystery celebrated with one's whole person'.

# 3: Where did it come from? The organic development of the liturgy

In its discussion of liturgical reform, the Second Vatican Council's Constitution on the Liturgy, *Sacrosanctum Concilium*, demanded (among other things) that 'care must be taken that any new forms adopted should in some way grow organically from forms already existing'.[46] The phrase 'organic development' is often used in discussions of the liturgy, and it will be useful to give some idea of how the liturgy has, in fact, developed through history.

It must first be noted how little we know of the earliest liturgy. The earliest liturgical books which have survived to the present day are from the seventh century. Into this gap of detailed knowledge it is very tempting for scholars to place what they would like to see, or to extend their favoured principles of development, such as 'the more complex derives from the less complex', backwards in time, without any real justification.

However, the Christian liturgy did not begin with a clean slate. It is based on three sources. The first is the Last Supper, which is connected to the liturgy by the Gospels and by St Paul. The Synoptic Gospels are clear that this was a Passover meal (e.g. Matthew 26:17-19), which had its own ritual. The second is the liturgy of the Synagogue, in which Jesus and his disciples all took part (e.g. Luke 4:21), which consisted of readings from Scripture, prayers, and teaching from a rabbi.

The third is the liturgy of the Temple, in which, again, our Lord and the disciples took part (e.g. John 7:14). This was the scene of complex ceremonial undertaken by a special class of priests and levites, wearing special clothes, with a calendar of seasons and sacrifices, feasts and fasts, over the year. The importance of the Temple liturgy in the thinking of the earliest Christians is attested by the Letter to the Hebrews and the Apocalypse of St John. The letter places great stress on the sacrificial priest entering through the veil that separates the Faithful from the Holy of Holies, and presents Christ the High Priest as accomplishing this passage definitively (see Hebrews 8–10, and *passim*). In the Apocalypse, the Temple's example lies behind the description of the liturgy of heaven, with its altar, the sacrificed Lamb, clouds of incense, ritual exclamations, and prostrations (see Revelation 7:9-12, 8:3, and *passim*).

While we don't know in any detail how the earliest liturgy was conducted, the liturgy we see recorded in the earliest liturgical books which we do have combine these three influences. A number of features of later liturgy have not yet emerged in these books, but that does not mean the Mass they describe is simple; indeed, by then it may have been influenced by another source, the ceremonial of Imperial Rome. Certainly, when the time of persecution was over, Christians were quick to adopt the model of the civic meeting hall, the basilica (literally, 'king's house'), for churches.

Analysis of literary style suggests that certain liturgical texts go back much further than the bound volumes in which they are preserved. The Roman Canon is generally regarded as having been composed (and not translated from a Greek original) at the end of the fourth century; the 'Intercessions' (*Orationes sollemnes*) of the Good Friday Liturgy seem to be still older, echoing the language of St Clement of Rome,[47] who was Pope until his death in the year 99. The tone and content of these most ancient of liturgical texts anticipates the *gravitas* and the theological concerns of the Extraordinary Form as it is experienced today, and in which they are still found.

There were several kinds of process through which the liturgy developed.

In the early centuries, there was a great deal of liturgical variation between places, and the history of the liturgy is in large part a history of the mutual influence of different liturgical traditions. The Frankish Emperor Charlemagne (who died in 814), whose advisors included the scholar Alcuin of York, was concerned that errors had crept into the liturgical texts and copies of the Bible in his dominions, and had the most highly-regarded books brought in from Rome, to be copied and used; expert singers were also brought in to pass on the Roman style of chant.

The liturgical volume Charlemagne was sent, a 'Sacramentary' today known as the 'Hadrianum', brought the liturgy of Rome to the whole of Christian France and Germany, but it did not include everything which was needed, and so was supplemented by local 'Gallican' texts. This created a fusion of the Roman and Gallican traditions.

Later, in the tenth century, it was Rome where, for various reasons, the need was felt to correct and augment the liturgical books locally available with the best which could be found elsewhere. This was a volume known as the 'Romano-Germanic Pontifical', which came from Metz. This served to bring texts of non-Roman origin into the Roman tradition.

On a smaller scale, ceremonies or texts which were well-established in one location could be incorporated into the liturgy of another. The freedom with which this could happen is illustrated by advice given by Pope Gregory the Great to St Augustine of Canterbury, about what liturgical books to use in England, where he had arrived in the year 597:

> Select from the Churches whatever things are devout, religious, and right; and when you have bound them, as it were, into a sheaf, let the minds of the English grow accustomed to it. [48]

In a similar way, texts and ceremonies once used only in a restricted context could be used in a wider context. An example is the *Gloria*, originally specific to Christmas, but later used for joyful feasts throughout the year, and on Sundays outside Advent and Lent.

In these ways, there was a mutual influence among different liturgical rites and usages in the West, and sometimes also influences from the East, as with the adoption of the feasts of Candlemas and the Transfiguration. This kind of development was a matter of supplementing or replacing one's local books with things of great prestige from elsewhere.

Some other processes of liturgical development should also be mentioned. One is that when new circumstances demanded it, new or adapted texts and ceremonies would be adopted.

An example would be the development of the Christian monarchies, which led to the development of coronation liturgies. Another developing need was the increasing desire of the Faithful to see the Blessed Sacrament during the Consecration, which led to the development of the Elevation. Another kind of need derived from the problems experienced with the most ancient form of the Kiss of Peace, which led to the development of the Paxbrede (an object which is kissed, by the celebrant and then by each member of the congregation in turn),[49] and later the restriction of the Kiss to those in the Sanctuary.

In these ways the liturgy adapted to the evolving circumstances of the times. It did so also in another way: in relation to the liturgical resources available.

For example, in the ninth century Low Mass – Mass celebrated by a priest alone, without deacon or subdeacon – developed for situations in which those assistants were not always available, notably when priests in monasteries, and later in parishes, wished to celebrate a daily Mass. Without the deacon or subdeacon, the ceremonies had to be quite drastically cut down. By contrast, in Cathedrals the abundance of available clergy and singers led to the development of ceremonies involving more and more of them.

In a similar way, St Francis decided to adopt the liturgy of the Papal Court for his own order. This implied a degree of adaptation to the circumstances the Friars would find themselves in all over Christendom. The extremely happy result of this adaptation, the thirteenth century '*Missale Romano-Seraphicum*', is the direct ancestor of the Extraordinary Form as celebrated today: a version of the Papal liturgy which can be celebrated in parish churches, on battlefields and on missions, as well as in great cathedrals.

These forms of liturgical development are essentially conservative in nature, the driving force being the authenticity, antiquity, and prestige of ceremonies and texts being adopted by one tradition from another. Even when new or adapted texts and ceremonies were needed, they took their inspiration from what precedents existed.

Thus Christian kings, starting with the Merovingians (or the early Scottish kings, if Adamnan's *Life of St Columba* is to be believed), were anointed like the kings of the Old Testament. Where brevity and simplicity were demanded for practical reasons, the fuller and more complex ceremony would often be alluded to, or included in symbolic, telescoped form. At Low Mass there is no deacon and subdeacon to receive the celebrant's blessing and carry the Gospel solemnly, with candles and incense, across the sanctuary, to be proclaimed towards the north, symbol of the yet-unconverted world: yet the priest uses almost the same words to ask God's blessing, and the Missal is transferred with some ceremony from the south to the north end of the altar by the server, where it is placed at an angle to face a little towards the north, rather that directly towards the liturgical east.

Over time, the prestige of the Roman liturgy itself led to the spread of the Roman Rite at the expense of local rites and usages. The adoption of the Roman Rite by the Franciscans was a key moment in this process: from then on, the Roman Rite was to be heard all over Europe. The historical and cultural importance of local rites was not entirely neglected, however. More than once the people of Milan successfully opposed attempts to suppress their own venerable 'Ambrosian' Rite (named after St Ambrose of Milan); the 'Mozarabic' Rite of Spain was carefully preserved, if only for use in two locations; and many of the great religious orders preserved their own liturgical books: the Dominicans, the Norbertines, the Carmelites, and the Cistercians. Pope Pius V, in his Bull *Quo Primum* (1570), demanded that local usages of any real age – two hundred years – should continue to be followed unless the Cathedral Chapter (or the General Chapter of a religious order) and the bishop (or superior) both agreed to adopt the Roman Rite. The Gallican Rites of France, the various rites of the British Isles, and the rites of Germany, eventually ceased to be used, but this was an extremely slow process, complete only in the mid- to late nineteenth century.

Although the different Missals used in the Western Church have a great deal in common, at the eve of the Second Vatican Council the Western Church was not characterised by uniformity in liturgical matters, to say nothing of the Eastern Rites, which were celebrated wherever Eastern clergy and Faithful were to be found.

The Council of Trent ordered a careful examination of the Roman books, with a view to their correction. Missals from the fourteenth and fifteenth centuries were duly consulted and where texts had been corrupted, they were restored to their original form.

At Trent, the use of Latin and the ceremonies of the Catholic liturgy were defended with great eloquence against Protestant objections. Notably, the Council Fathers taught:

> And whereas such is the nature of man, that, without external helps, he cannot easily be raised to the

meditation of divine things; therefore has holy Mother Church instituted certain rites, to wit that certain things be pronounced in the mass in a low, and others in a louder, tone. She has likewise employed ceremonies, such as mystic benedictions, lights, incense, vestments, and many other things of this kind, derived from an apostolical discipline and tradition, whereby both the majesty of so great a sacrifice might be recommended, and the minds of the Faithful be excited, by those visible signs of religion and piety, to the contemplation of those most sublime things which are hidden in this sacrifice. [50]

The errors opposed by Trent again became an issue in the seventeenth and eighteenth centuries, with attempts, influenced by the Jansenist heresy, to create an 'Enlightenment' liturgy, in the vernacular, with simplified ceremonies, no silence, and the people saying 'Amen' after each prayer of the Canon. This took its most comprehensive form under the Emperor Joseph II of Austria (1741–1790), whose liturgical innovations (which lacked any authorisation from the Holy See) were accompanied by a ferocious persecution of the contemplative religious orders in his domains. It was also during this era that the Jesuits, who were among the most effective opponents of this project, were expelled from many countries, and even suppressed by Pope Clement VIII in 1773, under intense pressure from supposedly Catholic monarchs.

In one of the great ironies of history, the era of the 'Enlightened Despots' who had caused the Church such grief was brought to an end by Napoleon and his eventual defeat. This ushered in a period of unprecedented restoration, of church buildings, Catholic schools, and monasticism, with a renewed interest in the Church's liturgy, leading to the studies of the 'Liturgical Movement', and the revival of Gregorian Chant. Even the Jesuits were revived, in 1814.

The only lasting legacy of this post-Tridentine era was the rewriting of some hymns in a more classical Latin style, which entered the Roman Breviary in 1631. Much later there was a similar attempt to classicise the Latin Psalter, in a version published in 1947, and which has left some traces in the Extraordinary Form. Neither of these revisions were adopted by the monastic orders, and the Second Vatican Council criticised them both.[51] By the time of that Council, however, other liturgical reforms were afoot.

## 4: Is it allowed? The legal status of the Extraordinary Form today

### After the Second Vatican Council

When revising the Breviary (today known as the Liturgy of the Hours) in 1910, Pope Pius X referred to plans for a more comprehensive liturgical reform. This plan of reform was again noted when the liturgies of Holy Week were revised in 1955, and was taken as one of the aims of the Second Vatican Council. Both of those earlier reforms were quite radical, and the reform which eventually emerged after the Council, in 1969, matched this ambition, this time applied to the whole Missal, after several years of incremental changes and unofficial liturgical experimentation.

Usually, upon its official promulgation, a new edition of the Roman Missal (or any other missal) automatically replaces the earlier edition of the Missal, the use of which is no longer allowed. This process is called 'obrogation'. In a different way, if the Pope wished to suppress a particular Missal – a local one, for example – he could decree its 'abrogation': the use of it would thereafter be legally forbidden.

The liturgical changes of the 1960s were the cause of considerable controversy. In particular, groups of the laity established themselves, from as early as 1964, to defend the principles of the older Missal. After 1969, they consistently used the argument that the 1962 Missal had not been obrogated, because the 1969 Missal was so different from the 1962 (despite having the same name: *Missale Romanum*) that it could not simply be regarded as the next edition in a long line of editions, but was instead something new. The older line of Missals had behind it both the force of long-standing custom, and the decree of Pope Pius V that the Missal approved by the Council of Trent could be used by priests 'in perpetuity'.[52]

One way of settling the matter, or trying to do so, would have been for Pope Paul VI or his successors to issue a decree of abrogation, or an authoritative clarification that the new Missal had obrogated the old. Repeated requests for such statements were rejected, however, as Annibale Bugnini, the architect of the liturgical reform, explains, out of a desire to avoid anything which would 'cast odium on the liturgical tradition'.[53] The most which was done was a 'note' from the Congregation for Divine Worship in 1974, which said that while bishops could allow older priests to celebrate the former Mass, they could not permit its celebration with a congregation.

By this time, however, things had already moved on. In 1971 Cardinal John Heenan, Archbishop of Westminster, had handed to Pope Paul VI a petition organised by the Latin Mass Society requesting that the use of the former Missal be allowed. The petition was signed by an international group of cultural figures, many of them non-Catholic, including Members of Parliament from each of the main British parties, two Anglican bishops, and many writers, poets, and musicians. The petition presented the case that the ancient Latin Mass had cultural value for the whole world, and its disappearance would be an incalculable loss.

Pope Paul responded positively to this petition, although this took the form of an 'indult' – a permission, or an exception to a general law – which was applicable only to England and Wales. The presence of the famous crime-writer Agatha Christie among the petitioners has given rise to this being called the 'Agatha Christie Indult'. In 1974, the Bishops' Conference of England and Wales adopted the principle that Catholics requesting the 1962 Mass for their funerals should be granted it.

In 1984, another indult for the celebration of the 1962 Missal was issued by Pope John Paul II, this time for the whole world,[54] and the same was reiterated in 1988.[55] All three indults stated that these Masses needed the permission of the local bishop. It became the task of the local groups of laity already mentioned, the Latin Mass Society in England and Wales and similar groups around the world, to ask bishops for such permissions, in a cottage industry of letter-writing, seeking out priests able and willing to celebrate the older Mass, and maintaining the skills (such as serving and singing) and equipment (such as suitable vestments) necessary for celebrations. The Latin Mass Society quickly developed a network of 'representatives' around the country, and in time a London office and paid staff, to undertake this work.

The restrictive nature of these permissions, however, was a source of frustration for many Catholics attached to the Extraordinary Form, and apparently also to Pope John Paul II, who described his 1988 document as establishing the 'necessary measures to guarantee respect for their rightful aspirations', and called on bishops to assist him: 'respect must everywhere be shown for the feelings of all those who are attached to the Latin liturgical tradition, by a wide and generous application of the directives already issued'.[56]

This difficult situation persisted for many years. Cardinal Joseph Ratzinger, then the Prefect of the Congregation for the Doctrine of the Faith, observed in a book published in 2000:

> Anyone who nowadays advocates the continuing existence of this liturgy or takes part in it is treated like a leper; all tolerance ends here. There has never been anything like this in history; in doing this we are despising and proscribing the Church's whole past. How can one trust her at present if things are that way?[57]

This strange, and, it must be said, unjust, situation was also the backdrop of a particular drama: that of Archbishop Lefebvre and his Society of St Pius X.

## Archbishop Lefebvre and the SSPX

Archbishop Marcel Lefebvre (1905-1991), a native of France, was a member of the Holy Ghost Fathers, a missionary order, and became Archbishop of Dakar (1955-1962), in Senegal, and briefly Bishop of Tulle in France (1962), before being elected as the Superior General of his order (1962-1968). He was an assistant in the preparations for the Second Vatican Council, and was subsequently a Council Father, and a leading figure in the grouping of more conservative bishops at the Council, the *Coetus Internationalis Patrum* ('International Group of Fathers').

After retiring from his leadership of the Holy Ghost Fathers, he was approached by seminarians dissatisfied with the training they were receiving, who asked him to set up a seminary where a more traditional formation would be possible. He did so in 1969 with the permission of the bishop of Fribourg in Switzerland, and this was the beginning of a priestly society, the Society of St Pius X.

As time went on, Archbishop Lefebvre came increasingly into conflict with the Roman authorities, until by the mid 1970s he was training and also ordaining priests without canonical approval. Early on the Archbishop had come to the conclusion that the 1962 Missal was indispensable to his project to form priests in the traditional manner, and it was this Missal which his priests used when they established apostolates, without reference to local bishops, around Europe, North America, and in time all over the world.

In 1988 an attempt was made to bring the SSPX back into the fold, and concessions in relation to the Extraordinary Form were part of the discussions which took place. These negotiations ultimately failed, however, and the Archbishop, conscious that he was nearing the end of his life, consecrated four of his priests bishops, with a like-minded bishop, Castro de Mayer of Campos, Brazil, as his co-consecrator. (Bishops, who alone can ordain priests, must themselves be ordained or 'consecrated' by two bishops, in a chain of ordinations leading back, ultimately, to the Twelve Apostles.)

A version of the concessions offered to Archbishop Lefebvre were incorporated into Pope John Paul II's 1988 indult, *Ecclesia Dei Adflicta*. In particular, members of the SSPX who disagreed with Archbishop Lefebvre's defiance of Rome were allowed to form their own priestly institute, also committed to the use of the 1962 Missal: the Priestly Fraternity of St Peter (FSSP). Other institutes and religious communities attached to this liturgy have been set up since then, and other groups and communities, once allied to the SSPX, have been given canonical status by the Holy See.

The SSPX, in the meantime, had been informed that the Archbishop and the men he had consecrated bishops were automatically excommunicated. Archbishop Lefebvre died in 1991, but since then attempts to reconcile the SSPX, as a body, to the Holy See, have not ceased. It was part of the motivation for Pope Benedict's later Apostolic Letter, *Summorum Pontificum*, in 2007 (to be discussed next). In 2009 Pope Benedict formally lifted the excommunication of the four SSPX bishops who had been consecrated in 1988. In 2015, the then General Superior of the SSPX, Bishop Bernard Fellay, was appointed 'judge of first instance' by the Prefect of the Congregation for the Doctrine of the Faith, to oversee the canonical trial of one of his own priests. In 2016, Pope Francis gave priests of the SSPX faculties to hear confessions – the liceity and validity of their confessions had been called into question up to then – and in 2017 he made arrangements for priests of the SSPX, like other clergy, to be able to be 'delegated' by a parish priest to witness marriages.

The SSPX today operates in countries all over the world, without oversight from local bishops, and in a somewhat ambiguous position. This ambiguity derives from the actions of successive Popes who, rather than wishing to harden divisions, have sought to create the conditions in which the SSPX can be reintegrated into the structures of the Church, and indeed, to start the process of doing so. How this situation will continue to develop is impossible, at present, to know.

## *Summorum Pontificum*

In 2007 Pope Benedict published a much-anticipated document, an Apostolic Letter 'given motu proprio' – 'of his own initiative' – which transformed the situation of the Extraordinary Form.

The 'Letter to Bishops' which accompanied it gave a very frank and extended explanation of the reasons for the document, which deserves to be quoted at length.

> [After the liturgical reform] it soon became apparent that a good number of people remained strongly attached to this [older] usage of the Roman Rite, which had been familiar to them from childhood. This was especially the case in countries where the liturgical movement had provided many people with a notable liturgical formation and a deep, personal familiarity with the earlier Form of the liturgical celebration. We all know that, in the movement led by Archbishop Lefebvre, fidelity to the old Missal became an external mark of identity; the reasons for the break which arose over this, however, were at a deeper level. Many people who clearly accepted the binding character of the Second Vatican Council, and were faithful to the Pope and the Bishops, nonetheless also desired to recover the form of the sacred liturgy that was dear to them. This occurred above all because in many places celebrations

were not faithful to the prescriptions of the new Missal, but the latter actually was understood as authorising or even requiring creativity, which frequently led to deformations of the liturgy which were hard to bear. I am speaking from experience, since I too lived through that period with all its hopes and its confusion. And I have seen how arbitrary deformations of the liturgy caused deep pain to individuals totally rooted in the faith of the Church. ...

Immediately after the Second Vatican Council it was presumed that requests for the use of the 1962 Missal would be limited to the older generation which had grown up with it, but in the meantime it has clearly been demonstrated that young persons too have discovered this liturgical form, felt its attraction and found in it a form of encounter with the Mystery of the Most Holy Eucharist, particularly suited to them.[58] Thus the need has arisen for a clearer juridical regulation which had not been foreseen at the time of the 1988 Motu Proprio. ...

I now come to the positive reason which motivated my decision to issue this Motu Proprio updating that of 1988. It is a matter of coming to an interior reconciliation in the heart of the Church. Looking back over the past, to the divisions which in the course of the centuries have rent the Body of Christ, one continually has the impression that, at critical moments when divisions were coming about, not enough was done by the Church's leaders to maintain or regain reconciliation and unity. One has the impression that omissions on the part of the Church have had their share of blame for the fact that these divisions were able to harden. This glance at the past imposes an obligation on us today: to make every effort to enable for all those who truly desire unity to remain in that unity or to attain it anew. I think of a sentence in the Second Letter to the Corinthians, where Paul writes: 'Our mouth is open to you, Corinthians; our heart is wide. You are not restricted by us, but you are restricted in your own affections. In return…widen your hearts also!' (2 Co 6:11-13). Paul was certainly speaking in another context, but his exhortation can and must touch us too, precisely on this subject. Let us generously open our hearts and make room for everything that the faith itself allows.

There is no contradiction between the two editions of the Roman Missal. In the history of the liturgy there is growth and progress, but no rupture. What earlier generations held as sacred, remains sacred and great for us too, and it cannot be all of a sudden entirely forbidden or even considered harmful. It behoves all of us to preserve the riches which have developed in the Church's faith and prayer, and to give them their proper place.

Pope Benedict felt very keenly the suffering of Catholics attached to the Extraordinary Form, and also the urgency of healing the division in the Church which had developed *vis-à-vis* the Society of St Pius X. In addition, however, and not to be minimised, is his feeling that the freeing of the older form of the Mass was in any case the right thing to do. There was something unnatural about restricting the Extraordinary Form, and doing so created a breach, not only between Catholics today, but between the Catholics of today and those of the past. As he had noted when a cardinal, repudiation of the past puts an institution's future into doubt. And finally, this form of the Mass has value: its availability will help Catholics grow in virtue.

It should also be noted that the Extraordinary Form had become involved in a theological debate, in which it was seen, by both sides, as standing aside from developments at and following the Second Vatican Council. Official negotiations between the SSPX and the Holy See had the clarification of doctrinal principles, as well as the liturgy, in view. Annibale Bugnini suggested that it was the theological positions of some of those who supported the Extraordinary Form which put Pope Paul VI off a more generous permission of it.[59] As a Cardinal, Joseph Ratzinger saw the matter from a contrasting perspective:

It is only against this background of the effective denial of the authority of Trent, that the bitterness of the struggle against allowing the celebration of Mass according to the 1962 Missal, after the liturgical reform, can be understood. The possibility of so celebrating constitutes the strongest, and thus (for them) the most intolerable contradiction of the opinion of those who believe that the faith in the Eucharist formulated by Trent has lost its value.[60]

The various issues involved in these debates cannot be entered into in this booklet, but it forms the background to Pope Benedict's appeal that bishops, and all Catholics, 'make room for everything that the faith itself allows': while theological debates continue, these should not impede the recovery of the Church's liturgical patrimony.

The legal means Pope Benedict chose to 'free' the Extraordinary Form was to say, first, that it had never been abrogated: 'I would like to draw attention to the fact that this Missal was never juridically abrogated and, consequently, in principle, was always permitted.'

Second, the 1962 Missal is to be regarded as an 'Extraordinary Form' or 'use' of the Roman Rite, whereas the reformed Mass is the 'Ordinary Form'.

This vindicated the longstanding argument of the defenders of the EF that it had always been a legitimate liturgical form, available to priests of the Western Church. However, *Summorum Pontificum* is above all a legal document, and these claims must be seen primarily as legal enactments. Pope Benedict was not, or not merely, making a contribution to an ongoing debate about the status of the 1962 Missal. He was making it true, by legal fiat, that it is not abrogated, and also that it is an Extraordinary Form of the Roman Rite.

What does the term 'Extraordinary Form' mean? It is a new term for the unusual status of the 1962 Missal, but it makes use of the idea that the Roman Rite can have different 'forms' or 'uses', such as those of geographical areas or religious orders. The Sarum and Gallican Missals, formerly used in much of the British Isles and France, for example, are best understood as versions of the Roman Rite, and not really as separate rites. The legal significance of this distinction is that whereas priests ordained in the Eastern Churches in communion with Rome do not automatically have the right to use the Roman Missal, and Western priests cannot normally use Eastern rites, the Council of Trent said that all priests ordained in the Western Church can celebrate the Roman Rite. In this case, the point is that the Extraordinary Form can be used by any priest of the Western Church, because, even if he was ordained in the Ordinary Form, the Extraordinary Form is simply a different 'form' of his own Rite.

It follows from *Summorum Pontificum* that priests do not need the permission of their bishops (or other superiors) to celebrate the EF, and that they can do so with congregations. The Extraordinary Form is in this way in the same position as the Ordinary Form.

In another way, however, it is given a special status: the Faithful may request celebrations, whether one-off Masses or regular ones, and the rectors of churches and bishops are directed to fulfil such requests. There may, of course, be practical obstacles (a lack of priests able to celebrate it, or churches for the celebrations to take place), but the principle is clear. The Faithful who are denied the Extraordinary Form are directed to refer the matter to Rome, where a special office (now the Fourth Section of the Congregation for the Doctrine of the Faith), is tasked with assisting the bishop in making the Extraordinary Form available.

## After *Summorum Pontificum*

The consequences of *Summorum Pontificum* were very noticeable. Over the following three years, the number of Sunday EF Masses celebrated in England and Wales doubled; similar rates of growth can be seen elsewhere. Furthermore, it began to be celebrated occasionally by a growing number of bishops, and there has developed far greater official involvement in events involving the Extraordinary Form, such as the great Paris to Chartres pilgrimage organised by Notre Dame de Chretienté.

Particularly noticeable is the increasing number of apostolates (chapels, parishes, and so on) of the priestly institutes committed to the Extraordinary Form, and the willingness of the bishops where these are located to carry out priestly ordinations for those institutes, using the older version of the Pontifical (the book of bishop's liturgies), a very vivid sign of the increasing acceptance and integration of the EF into the life of the Church at a local level.

While it never actually disappeared completely, the celebration of what is now called the Extraordinary Form was at a very low ebb in the 1970s and 1980s. Despite rapid growth more recently, it still represents a very small percentage of the Masses being celebrated in a typical diocese, and will continue to be a minority interest for the foreseeable future. The next two chapters consider the movement which has grown up around it, and the place it has in the life of the Church.

# 5: Who supports it? The movement for the Extraordinary Form

As I have already quoted him, Cardinal Ratzinger noted at the beginning of the new millennium that the supporter of the Extraordinary Form 'is treated like a leper'. It is not surprising, therefore, that the early lay leaders of the movement to preserve the Extraordinary Form were men and women of great independence and moral courage.

Two Germans were perhaps the most important. The first, Dr Eric de Saventhem (1919–2005), led the *Foederatio Internationalis Una Voce* (FIUV, or Una Voce International), from 1967 until 1994; the second was the philosopher, Dietrich von Hildebrand (1889–1977). Both came from cultivated backgrounds, and both had been determined opponents of Adolf Hitler. Saventhem had managed to defect to the British from the German Embassy in Istanbul in 1944; Hildebrand had to flee from Vienna when the Germans invaded Austria in 1938, because of his work as editor of an anti-Nazi newspaper. Both men later used their considerable talents and extensive contacts in the cause of the Extraordinary Form, Saventhem making the case for it in Rome on behalf of the international movement, and Hildebrand, by then based in the United States of America, laying the philosophical and theological foundations for its defence in two influential books: *Trojan Horse in the City of God* (1969) and *Devastated Vineyard* (1973).

Both men were also converts to Catholicism, and it is remarkable how many converts are among the most prominent defenders of the Extraordinary Form. In England, the unofficial leader of the movement, until his early death, was the convert and novelist Evelyn Waugh (1903–1966); his poignant correspondence with Cardinal John Heenan, the Archbishop of Westminster, on the liturgical reform, has been published as a short book.[61] The Latin Mass Society's early years were dominated by two other converts, the apologist and skiing pioneer Sir Arnold Lunn (1888–1974), and the former Anglican clergyman, theologian, and writer Hugh Ross-Williamson (1901–1978).

A little later, another convert, the prolific Michael Treharne Davies (1936–2004), a teacher by profession, presented the case for the Extraordinary Form to a whole generation through his highly readable, carefully researched, and much-translated books, most famously *Pope John's Council* (1977) and *Pope Paul's New Mass* (1980).

The Extraordinary Form has always been strongly supported by many artists and writers. Among the signatories of the 'Agatha Christie' petition to Pope Paul VI we find the Catholic writers Malcolm Muggeridge and Compton Mackenzie, and the artist and poet David Jones, alongside many non-Catholics. Other Catholic writers with a special fondness for the Extraordinary Form include the contrasting figures of J.R.R. Tolkien and Graham Greene. The Latin Mass Society has had two internationally-recognised Catholic composers among its Patrons: the late Colin Mawby and Sir James Macmillan.

Important as this intellectual leadership has been, the movement for the Extraordinary Form would not have developed as it did were it not for the commitment of a great many ordinary Catholics: people sometimes dismissed as too ignorant to appreciate the reformed Mass, or even in thrall to superstition,[62] but actually, in the words of Pope Benedict, 'individuals totally rooted in the faith of the Church'. For them, the ancient Mass, with its distinctive atmosphere and its spirituality, was central to their sense of the Faith. As Pope Benedict also observed, it had been assumed that the phenomenon of the strong attachment of so many of the 'simple Faithful' to the old, familiar liturgical forms, was a problem which would disappear with their generation, but as time has shown, the Extraordinary Form has also come to be appreciated by young people and others new to the Faith.

Two other features of the movement should be noted. One is that, because most people who have attended the Extraordinary Form over the years have had to travel to do so, congregations tend to be more representative of the Church as a whole – in terms of educational backgrounds, class and ethnicity – than is sometimes the case in parishes, where people are drawn from a small geographical area, and can shop around between parishes and among Masses within parishes.

The other feature is that those Catholics attached to the Extraordinary Form who have over the years attended Masses approved by the bishops, as opposed to Masses offered by the SSPX, have done so in a conscious effort to maintain their connection with their bishops and the Holy Father, sometimes at considerable personal cost. The work of the Una Voce movement, including the Latin Mass Society, has always been to facilitate Masses within the 'structures of the Church', because the visible unity of the Church was and is regarded as paramount. Even while making the case that permission for celebrating the Extraordinary Form was not necessary – an argument finally vindicated in 2007 – the movement devoted itself to getting permissions: a policy which appears now, with hindsight, as a matter of supererogatory obedience.

# 6: What is it for? The place of the Extraordinary Form in the Church

## Liturgical and spiritual pluralism

As has already been indicated, there is no intrinsic problem about the Church as a whole, or the Western Church in particular, having multiple liturgical forms. This has been the norm throughout history, and as the Second Vatican Council taught:

> Even in the liturgy, the Church has no wish to impose a rigid uniformity in matters which do not implicate the faith or the good of the whole community.[63]

Nevertheless, if the Extraordinary Form is to have a place in the life of the Church, it should be justified in terms of its contribution to the Church's mission: the salvation of souls and the glorification of God. If it can bring people to Faith, and strengthen and sustain those already there, then there can be no objection to it.

That it does do so is indicated in the words of Pope Benedict already quoted: that there are those who find the Extraordinary Form 'particularly suited to them', and that, more simply still, it represents 'riches'.

A partial parallel can be seen with the relationship between the liturgies of the West and the East. The Second Vatican Council's decree on Ecumenism explained:

> In the study of revelation East and West have followed different methods, and have developed differently their understanding and confession of God's truth. It is hardly surprising, then, if from time to time one tradition has come nearer to a full appreciation of some aspects of a mystery of revelation than the other, or has expressed it to better advantage. In such cases, these various theological expressions are to be considered often as mutually complementary rather than conflicting.[64]

In a similar way, the things which the Extraordinary Form can teach us take nothing away from the Ordinary Form.

Other partial parallels would be with the schools of spirituality found in the Church – Ignatian, Benedictine, Dominican and so on – and with the New Movements. The Extraordinary Form certainly has a distinct flavour, although nothing as fully worked-out as Ignatian spirituality, which builds upon liturgical spirituality, let alone the all-encompassing spiritual programme of one of the New Movements. If alternative spiritual schools are allowed, then even more so must room be found for the spiritual tradition represented by the Extraordinary Form. This is, after all, simply the spiritual tradition of the Church's liturgy up to 1964, and this cannot be said to be in conflict with the teaching of the Church. In the words of Pope Benedict, already quoted: 'Let us generously open our hearts and make room for everything that the faith itself allows.'

## Who is attracted to the Extraordinary Form?

Why should anyone gain particular insight or inspiration from the Extraordinary Form? The outlines of an answer to this question have already been given in the opening chapter of this booklet. The EF communicates to the worshipper in a way somewhat distinct from the mode employed by the Ordinary Form. Whereas the OF primarily uses words, the EF uses a wide range of means, with greater emphasis on dramatic ceremonial and the creation of a sense of the sacred: 'the sacrality which attracts many people to the former usage,' as Pope Benedict noted.[65]

The way that the Extraordinary Form conveys the sense of the sacred non-verbally can be particularly useful to those for whom the words of the liturgy are less effective at conveying the mystery of the Mass. Most obviously, this will include those less at ease with the language in which the Ordinary Form is celebrated, such as people who tend to hear Mass being celebrated in a second language, children, and males.

To consider these groups in reverse order, it has been shown that men are less verbally-orientated than women, and a very striking feature of the Extraordinary Form is that whereas in Britain and America men make up only about one in three of the typical Catholic congregation, in the Extraordinary Form congregations are typically slightly more than 50% men.

Small children seem to appreciate the atmosphere of the Extraordinary Form, and while evidence is only anecdotal, it is often said that even children not used to it are quieter and more recollected at a Mass which is itself quieter, and where there is an atmosphere of quiet for them to absorb and imitate. 'Children's liturgies' are not felt to be necessary at celebrations of the Extraordinary Form, and many congregations include an unusually large number of children.

Those obliged to hear Mass in a second language, or perhaps one not understood at all, will not reap the benefits offered by the Ordinary Form in terms of the immediate comprehension of the texts. This is true not only of many immigrants, but also of native speakers of many minority languages, a serious obstacle to a truly 'vernacular' liturgy, particularly in Africa and China.

These Catholics may also be attracted to the Extraordinary Form because its spirituality is more akin to the traditional spirituality of many cultures. This affinity has also been expressed by Jewish and Muslim converts, who are used to a more atmospheric, ritualised, form of worship, with the use of sacred languages and chant.

In a somewhat different way, it has also on occasion had a special appeal to those attracted to the New Age, who, as the late Stratford Caldecott expressed it in another CTS booklet, seek 'a *transforming contact* with mystery'.[66] Anyone put off by a rationalistic presentation of religion will find, in the Extraordinary Form (to repeat the words of Pope Benedict), 'a form of encounter with the Mystery of the Most Holy Eucharist, particularly suited to them.'

# 7: What else is there? The sacraments, sacramentals, Office, and devotions

There is more to the liturgy than the Mass, and there is more to the devotional life than the liturgy. The Extraordinary Form of the Mass stands at the centre of a liturgical and devotional system which offers many opportunities to experience closely related forms of prayer, which prepare for, develop, and deepen, a spiritual life with Mass at its centre.

## The other sacraments

*Summorum Pontificum* makes it clear that not only the Extraordinary Form of the Mass, but also the other sacraments found in the 'earlier ritual', may be offered to the Faithful by parish priests and (in the case of the Sacrament of Confirmation), by bishops.[67] Today the celebration of the Sacrament of Marriage in the EF is well-established, for example, and the Archdiocese of Westminster in England has a long-standing arrangement of providing an auxiliary bishop to confer the Sacrament of Confirmation at an annual service organised by the Latin Mass Society.

It is natural that those attached to the Extraordinary Form of Mass should seek the other sacraments in this form, as the ceremonies and prayers are very much in the same spirit.

For example, the Nuptial Blessing in the EF Wedding Service is a long and very beautiful prayer invoking a succession of blessings, specifically for the bride, who in the Pauline conception of marriage noted earlier is the 'body' of the husband and represents the family. The Ordinary Form version of this blessing has been made to apply to both parties, and divided into three sections, which are offered as alternatives to each other.

Similarly, in the Baptismal ceremony of the Extraordinary Form, there is a succession of exorcisms, recalling the exorcisms used in the early Church for converts from paganism, and vivid and dramatic rituals: the giving to the candidate of a tiny portion of salt, representing wisdom, and the opening of the candidate's ears and mouth, recalling our Lord's cure of the deaf and dumb man (Mark 7:33), and even using the same Aramaic word of command: 'ephphatha'.[68]

The ceremony of the rite of Confirmation, which is short, includes the vivid symbolic striking of each candidate's cheek by the bishop, recalling the *colée* of the medieval knighting ceremony.

# The Office

*Summorum Pontificum* extends priests' freedom to use the Extraordinary Form of the Mass to the use of the older version of the Breviary or Divine Office, called in the Ordinary Form the Liturgy of the Hours.[69] Even more freedom is afforded to the laity, who are 'earnestly invited' to pray the Office, though not obliged to do so. [70]

The Breviary is very closely related to the Missal: the collect for Lauds and Vespers on a Sunday is that of the day's Mass, and the Gospel passage read at Sunday Mass are commented on in the readings of that day's Matins. Other elements throughout the Office, such as antiphons, anticipate or hark back to the Mass of the day.

The beauty of the ancient Latin psalter and the chants used in the Office was praised in the strongest terms by Pope Paul VI, whose words in 1966, addressed to religious superiors, bear repeating:

> In present conditions, what words or melodies could replace the forms of Catholic devotion which you have used until now? You should reflect and carefully consider whether things would not be worse, should this fine inheritance be discarded. It is to be feared that the choral office would turn into a mere bland recitation, suffering from poverty and begetting weariness, as you yourselves would perhaps be the first to experience. One can also wonder whether men would come in such

numbers to your churches in quest of the sacred prayer, if its ancient and native tongue, joined to a chant full of grave beauty, resounded no more within your walls.[71]

The Office is the birth-right of the parish, as well as of the religious community. Noting the possibility that it can be sung by a priest with the laity, the Second Vatican Council describes it as:

truly the voice of the bride addressed to her bridegroom; it is the very prayer which Christ himself, together with his body, addresses to the Father. This expression of the Church's prayer should be reclaimed.[72]

The movement for the Extraordinary Form has answered this exhortation of the Second Vatican Council, and public, sung, celebrations especially of Vespers or Compline have become a feature of devotional events using the Extraordinary Form, where Mass is also celebrated.

In addition to the Roman Office, used by diocesan clergy and in parishes, and the various Offices celebrated by religious orders such as Benedictines, the Little Office of the Blessed Virgin Mary should also be mentioned. Commenting on its great popularity in the late Middle Ages, the historian Eamon Duffy comments:

The Little Hours included some of the most beautiful and accessible parts of the psalter, notably the gradual Psalms, whose humane and tender tone was accentuated by the Marian antiphons, lessons, and collects celebrating the beauty, goodness, and merciful kindness of the Virgin, with which the Office surrounded them. Offering the lay devotee some approximation to the order and tranquillity of monastic piety, it possessed the vital qualification for lay devotion of being relatively uncomplicated, varying very little with the liturgical seasons...[73]

There is no need to refer to it in the past tense, however: the Little Office is undergoing a great revival among Catholics attached to the Extraordinary Form, and today no fewer than three different editions are in print with an English facing translation.[74]

### Blessings and devotions

There are many blessings, processions and other services, most importantly the rite of Burial, as well as the sacraments of Baptism and Extreme Unction, contained in a separate liturgical book, the *Rituale Romanum*, and books derived from this.[75] The edition of the Ritual which corresponds to the 1962 Missal naturally conforms to it in spirit, and its contents have become a very popular complement to the liturgical life offered by the Extraordinary Form.

Brief blessings of objects, such as rosaries and devotional images, and house blessings, are perennially popular, but there are also important longer blessings included in the Ritual. The Blessing of a Woman After Childbirth ('Churching') is today often given immediately before or after the Baptism of a baby when that is celebrated in the Extraordinary Form. It is a very beautiful thanksgiving for childbirth as well as a blessing for the new mother. The Blessing of Pilgrims, before and after their pilgrimage, is also regularly used. These somewhat longer blessings generally include the singing or saying of an appropriate psalm, with an antiphon, followed by several short blessings focused on different aspects of the occasion.

The value of having blessed objects in one's house, such as palms from Palm Sunday, the use of blessed chalk at Epiphany, holy water, salt, and foodstuffs often blessed on a special feast-day,[76] and so on, is something which is being rediscovered in the context of the Extraordinary Form, as is the use of sacramentals such as the Brown Scapular and the Miraculous Medal, the veneration of relics, pilgrimages, and other traditional pious practices and devotions.

In 2001 the Congregation for Divine Worship published a *Directory of Popular Piety and the Liturgy* to encourage and regulate a great many traditional practices, lamenting the development, following the Second Vatican Council but certainly not mandated by it, of the 'manifest and hasty abandonment of inherited forms of popular piety resulting in a void not easily filled', and 'unjustified criticism of the piety of the common people'.[77] Popular piety is to be found today flourishing in particular among Catholics attached to the Extraordinary Form, and in the context of events organised around the celebration of the EF Mass. The *Directory* reiterates the key principle of pious practices, set out by the Second Vatican Council, which is observed in a very clear way in the context of the EF: that these practices be subordinated to the liturgy, be in accordance with its spirit and its seasons, and in no way come to seem a substitute for or distraction from it.[78] For Catholics attached to the Extraordinary Form, it is the liturgy, and above all the Mass, which is paramount.

## 8: What about the Reform of the Reform? The ongoing liturgical debate in the Church

Chapter 2 examined a number of features of the Extraordinary Form with a view to explaining their meaning and value. In several cases – most obviously the use of Latin, the priest facing East, and reception of Holy Communion kneeling and on the tongue – the Ordinary Form also allows the same or a very similar practice. It is unusual to find the Ordinary Form celebrated in Latin, facing East, and so on, but it is not unknown, and a movement exists to promote the celebration of the Ordinary Form in a way which makes it closer to the Extraordinary Form, and perhaps even to change some of the rules to allow an even closer approximation (allowing the Eucharistic Prayer to be said silently, for example). This is the movement for a 'Reform of the Reform': that is, to revisit or reform again the liturgical reform carried out following Vatican II.

Those attached to the Extraordinary Form are naturally sympathetic to arguments in favour of the use of Latin and other features more characteristic of the EF, but some caution is needed here. The Reform of the Reform movement developed at a time when celebration of the Extraordinary Form was very restricted, and one way of understanding it is as an alternative to the EF: if it seemed impossible to use the older Missal alongside the newer, then (some reasoned) perhaps the newer could be made closer to the older. It is not clear, therefore, whether the freeing of the Extraordinary Form strengthens the Reform of the Reform, because it appears to vindicate some of its key arguments, or weakens it, because it makes it unnecessary.

It would appear, for example, that the number of places where the Ordinary Form is celebrated in Latin has declined since *Summorum Pontificum* was published in 2007. On the other hand, it can happen that a priest wishing to introduce the Extraordinary Form will introduce certain features, such as the celebration of Mass *ad orientem*, to his celebration of the Ordinary Form, either in advance of adding the Extraordinary Form to the parish schedule, as a kind of preparation for it, or following this, because regular celebration of the EF has underlined for him the value of the practice. This last possibility seems to have been in the mind of Pope Benedict XVI when he wrote of the influence of the Extraordinary Form on the way the Ordinary Form is celebrated: 'The celebration of the Mass according to the Missal of Paul VI will be able to demonstrate, more powerfully than has been the case hitherto, the sacrality which attracts many people to the former usage.'[79]

Two further points should be borne in mind. The first is that, while discussing historical and pastoral issues arising from different parts of the Mass can be helpful, the

Reform of the Reform is about the best way to understand and develop, specifically, the *Ordinary* Form. Official documents implementing and commenting on the liturgical reform left certain issues unclear, and a lot of discussion revolves around what was really intended by the Fathers of the Second Vatican Council, and others involved.

This complex and occasionally heated debate, about how to understand and implement the liturgical reform correctly, is one in which Catholics attached to the Extraordinary Form have no need or desire to join.

The second point is that the Extraordinary Form is a package, whereas the Reform of the Reform tends to separate issues such as Latin, *ad orientem* worship, the manner of receiving Holy Communion, and so on, and deal with them individually.

There are two difficulties with this approach. One is that it leads to a debate within parishes and religious communities which seems destined to continue forever. The other is that things which make sense as part of a package do not necessarily work so well separately.

The Extraordinary Form represents an opportunity for parishes and religious communities to recover the 'riches' of the Church's liturgical patrimony, without necessarily changing what happens in the other Masses celebrated on Sundays and throughout the week. Typically, the Extraordinary Form is celebrated on a formerly free spot in the liturgical schedule, or one Ordinary Form Mass out of several is changed into an Extraordinary Form Mass. Nothing is taken away from those who wish to attend the Ordinary Form, while something is given to those who may wish to discover this other Form, which may be new to them. This should be done in a serene fashion which does not cause disruption or unnecessary upset.

# Conclusion

The proof of the pudding, as the saying has it, is in the eating. Observations from two recent events for young professionals in London, which included the celebration of a Sung Mass in the Extraordinary Form of the Roman Rite in one case, and of the traditional Dominican Rite in the other, supply some anecdotal evidence for how this liturgical tradition appears to people new to it.

Not everyone liked it, but those who felt motivated to use a feedback form to say so were few. The great majority recorded a positive response: the words 'solemn', 'beautiful', 'reverent', and 'prayerful' predominated. Others commented 'A charming experience', and 'So calm and pure'. One wrote: 'I feel so blessed to be able to see such a reverent Rite for Our Lord'.

The Diocese of Miami, Florida, records a story on its website about a young woman whose experience of the Extraordinary Form on a visit to England helped her find the Catholic Church.

Formerly an atheist, her aversion toward religion changed at the end of her college career, when she became a Protestant. During her post-collegiate travels she became resolute in converting to Catholicism after attending a *Missa Cantata*, or Sung Mass, in the parish of her favourite author, J.R.R. Tolkien,[80] a devout Catholic who penned *The Lord of the Rings* series. ...

When she heard Latin hymns coming from the choir loft, Tavakoli said, it felt like 'hearing angels on high.'

She was mesmerised. 'It truly is extraordinary,' she said. 'There is something beautiful and sacred about this form of the Mass.' [81]

Longstanding members of the movement which supports the Extraordinary Form know many such stories. Sometimes this Mass can reach people in a special way. The Extraordinary Form is not about forcing people to attend a Mass which does not suit them: it is about making possible a spiritual experience which some find helpful, and others life-changing.

# Further reading, organisations and resources

## Books

There is an immense literature on the history of the liturgy and the modern liturgical reform which is relevant to the Extraordinary Form. The following represents only a sample. First, some more personal recommendations.

**A short, step-by-step guide to the Extraordinary Form:**

Ronald Knox *The Mass in Slow Motion* (1948)
Many of the historical and theological claims in this booklet are argued at greater length in this work edited by the same author:

Joseph Shaw (ed.) *The Case for Liturgical Restoration: Una Voce Studies on the Traditional Latin Mass* (2019)
The most significant modern contribution to the debate on the liturgical reform:

Joseph Ratzinger *The Spirit of the Liturgy* (2000)
A particularly influential presentation of the rationale of the Extraordinary Form:

Martin Mosebach *The Heresy of Formlessness: The Roman Liturgy and its Enemy* (2006; revised and expanded edition, 2018)
A gentle introduction to the wider concerns of the movement for the Extraordinary Form:

Roger Buck: *The Gentle Traditionalist: A Catholic Fairy-tale from Ireland* (2015)
A book which guides the reader through the Mass in light of classical theological thinking about the liturgy:

Thomas Crean *The Mass and the Saints* (2009)

### a. Hand Missals

*Daily Missal 1962* (Baronius Press)

*St Andrew Daily Missal 1945* (St Bonaventure Publications)

Robert Power *Jesus Make Me Worthy* (Children's Missal)

*A Missal for Young Catholics* (Os Justi Press)

*Ordinary Prayers of the Traditional Latin Mass*
(Latin Mass Society)

### b. Liturgical Commentaries

*A commentary on the Ordinary of the Mass:*

James Jackson, FSSP, *Nothing Superfluous* (2016)

*Commentaries on the liturgical year:*

Prosper Guéranger *The Liturgical Year*

Ildefonsus Schuster *The Sacramentary*

Pius Parsch *The Church's Year of Grace*

Gueranger's *magnum opus* takes up fourteen small volumes, and is available online; the English translation has been reprinted. Parsch's work is a more manageable five volumes, but like Schuster's, is currently only available second-hand.

### c. Systematic histories of the Roman Rite

Adrian Fortescue *The Mass. A Study of the Roman Liturgy* (1912)

Josef Jungmann *Mass of the Roman Rite* (1948)

Archdale King *Liturgy of the Roman Church* (1957)

Alcuin Reid *The Organic Development of the Liturgy* (2005)

### d. On the Liturgical Reform

Ralph Wiltgen *The Rhine Flows into the Tiber: A History of Vatican II* (1967); republished as *The Inside Story of Vatican II* (1991)

Michael T. Davies *Pope John's Council* (1977; revised edition 2008)

Michael T. Davies *Pope Paul's New Mass* (1980; revised edition 2009)

Annibale Bugnini *The Reform of the Liturgy 1948-1975* (1990)

Aidan Nichols *Looking at the Liturgy* (1997)

Klaus Gamber *The Modern Rite* (2002) or his *The Reform of the Roman Liturgy: Its Problems and Background* (1993)

László Dobszay *The Restoration and Organic Development of the Roman Rite* (2010)

Peter Kwasniewski *Resurgent in the Midst of Crisis: Sacred Liturgy, the Traditional Latin Mass, and Renewal in the Church* (2014)

Peter Kwasniewski *Noble Beauty, Transcendent Holiness: Why the Modern Age Needs the Mass of Ages* (2017)

Yves Chiron *Annibale Bugnini: Reformer of the Liturgy* (2018)

### e. Specific Issues arising from the Reform

Hugh Ross Williamson: *The Great Prayer: Concerning the Canon of the Mass* (1956)

Christine Mohrmann *Liturgical Latin* (1959)

Uwe Michael Lang *Turning Towards the Lord: Orientation in Liturgical Prayer* (2009)

Bishop Juan Rodolfo Laise *Communion in the Hand* (2011; revised edition 2018)

Bishop Athanasius Schneider *Dominus Est: Reflections of a Bishop of Central Asia on Holy Communion* (2012)

Lauren Pristas *The Collects of the Roman Missals* (2012)

Matthew Hazell *Index Lectionum: A Comparative Table of Readings for the Ordinary and Extraordinary Forms of the Roman Rite* (2016)

### f. The Liturgical Reform in a Wider Context

Dietrich von Hildebrand *Trojan Horse in the City of God* (1969)

Dietrich von Hildebrand *Devastated Vineyard* (1973)

Anne Roche Muggeridge *Desolate City: Revolution in the Catholic Church* (1986)

Malachi Martin *The Jesuits* (1988)

Romano Amerio *Iota Unum: A Study of Changes in the Catholic Church in the Twentieth Century* (1996)

Ann Carey *Sisters in Crisis* (1997; new edition 2013)

H.J.A. Sire *Phoenix from the Ashes: The Making, Unmaking, and Restoration of Catholic Tradition* (2015)

### g. On the movement for the Extraordinary Form

Ronald Warwick *The Living Flame: The First Twenty-Five Years of the Society of St Pius X in Britain* (1997)

Bishop Bernard Tissier de Mallerais *Marcel Lefebvre: The Biography* (2004)

Leo Darroch *Una Voce: The History of the Foederatio Internationalis Una Voce* (2017)

### h. Fiction

Antonia Forest *The Attic Term* (1976)

Fr Bryan Houghton *Mitre and Crook* (1979)

Fr Bryan Houghton *Judith's Marriage* (1987)

Alice Thomas Ellis *The Sin Eater* (1986)

Stephen Oliver *Smoke in the Sanctuary* (2004)

Natalia Sanmartin Fenollera *The Awakening of Miss Prim* (2013)

## Organisations

### a. Lay Associations

*England and Wales*

Latin Mass Society *www.lms.org.uk*

Gregorian Chant Network *gregorianchantnetwork.blogspot.com*

Guild of St Clare *www.guildofstclare.org*

St Catherine's Trust *www.stcatherinestrust.org*

*Scotland*

Una Voce Scotland *www.unavoce-scotland.uk*

Confraternity of St Ninian *www.confraternity-of-st-ninian.com*

*Ireland*

Latin Mass Society of Ireland *www.latinmassireland.com*

*France*

Una Voce France *www.unavoce.fr*

Notre Dame to Chretienté (organiser of the Paris to Chartres walking pilgrimage) *www.nd-chretiente.com/index-eng.php*

*International*

Foederatio Internationalis Una Voce (Una Voce International)
*www.fiuv.org*

Foederatio Internationalis Juventutem (youth movement)
*www.juventutem.org*

Cœtus Internationalis Summorum Pontificum: organises the
Populus Summorum Pontificum Pilgrimage to Rome
*www.populussummorumpontificum.com*

For a full list of the members of the FIUV, see:
*www.fiuv.org/p/worldwide-member-associations.html*

## b. Priestly Institutes and Communities active in the British Isles

Fraternity of St Peter *www.fssp.co.uk*

Institute of Christ the King Sovereign Priest *www.icksp.org.uk*

Sons of the Most Holy Redeemer *www.papastronsay.com*

Silverstream Priory *www.cenacleosb.org*

Family of Mary Immaculate and St Francis
*www.stmarysgosport.org.uk*

## c. Specialist bookshops

Latin Mass Society Bookshop *www.lms.org.uk/shop*

St Philip's Books *www.stphilipsbooks.co.uk*

St Michael's Abbey Press *www.theabbeyshop.com*

Cenacle Catholic Books and Gifts *www.cenacle.co.uk*

Carmel Books *www.carmel-books.org*

### d. Other online resources

Fisheaters: the Whys and Hows of Traditional Catholicism
*www.fisheaters.com*

Thesaurus Preces Latinae *www.preces-latinae.org/index.htm*

The Divinum Officium Project *www.divinumofficium.com*

Gregorian Chant Network (UK based)
*gregorianchantnetwork.blogspot.com*

Catholic Music Association of America *www.musicasacra.com*

Corpus Christi Watershed *www.ccwatershed.org*

New Liturgical Movement *www.newliturgicalmovement.org*

### e. Smart Phone Apps

iMass (texts of Masses for the day and much more)

iPieta (EF and OF calendars and readings for Mass, and many other resources)

LiberPro (searchable scan of the *Liber Usualis*)

Traditional Ordo 2019 (liturgical calendar)

## A note about the Latin Mass Society

The author of this booklet is Chairman of the Latin Mass Society (LMS). Founded in 1965, the LMS is a membership organisation with a small London office and paid staff. It is a registered charity, number 248388.

It maintains a network of Local Representatives throughout England and Wales, meets regularly with representatives of the Bishops' Conference, and is an active member of the international federation of similar organisations around the world, the Foederatio Internationalis Una Voce (FIUV).

The Latin Mass Society facilitates the celebration of Masses in the Extraordinary Form throughout England and Wales, and organises many pilgrimages and devotional and educational activities. It organises training for priests who wish to celebrate the Extraordinary Form, for servers, and for singers of Gregorian Chant. It runs a residential Latin Course, and events for those who wish to make and restore traditional vestments. It supports an annual Summer School for children, run by the St Catherine's Trust. The LMS also maintains an online shop, and publishes a free quarterly magazine, *Mass of Ages*.

# Endnotes

[1] Fr Michel Sinoir *'La Question de l'Admission des Femmes au Service de l'Autel'* (Paris, Pierre Téqui, 1994).

[2] Apostolic Journey to Rio De Janeiro on the Occasion Of The XXVIII World Youth Day: Press Conference Of Pope Francis during the return flight, Sunday 28th July 2013.

[3] *Roman Pontifical*: formula used during the ordination of a priest.

[4] See the *Penny Catechism* 141.

[5] Article in *The Spectator*, 1964; reproduced in *A Bitter Trial* ed. Reid, pp40-41.

[6] *Mediator Dei* (1947): 108.

[7] Pope Pius X *Tra la Sollicitudini* (1907) 3.

[8] Second Vatican Council, Constitution on the Liturgy: *Sacrosanctum Concilium* (1962) 116.

[9] Pope John Paul II Apostolic Letter *Orientale Lumen* (1995) 11.

[10] See Thomas Crean *The Mass and the Saints* (Ignatius Press, 2008).

[11] The phrase occurs in the Roman Canon (Eucharistic Prayer).

[12] A fuller treatment of a larger number of such issues can be found in Joseph Shaw (ed), *The Case for Liturgical Restoration* (Angelico Press, 2019).

[13] Joseph Ratzinger *Spirit of the Liturgy* (Ignatius Press, 2000) p81.

[14] Related texts include Zechariah 3:8, Malachi 3:30m John 1:9, Psalm 67:34.

[15] Instruction *Il Padre, Incomprensibile* (1996) 107.

[16] Habakkuk 2:20.

[17] Joseph, Cardinal Ratzinger *The Spirit of the Liturgy* (San Francisco: Ignatius Press, 2000) pp215-216.

[18] Pope John Paul II, Apostolic Letter *Spiritus et Sponsa* (2003).

[19] Pope Benedict XVI: Message for the 46th World Communications Day "Silence and the Word: Path of Evangelisation" (2012).

[20] Congregation for Divine Worship, Instruction *Liturgiam Authenticam* (2001) 27.

[21] See Christine Mohrmann *Liturgical Latin* (Burns Oats, 1959).

[22] *Sacrificium Laudis* (1966).

[23] General Audience 26th November 1969.

[24] Pope John Paul II Apostolic Letter (1980) *Dominicae Cenae* 10.

[25] Pope John Paul II, Address to the Latinitas Foundation, 27th November 1978.

[26] Matthew 24:15-35; Mark 13:14ff; Daniel 9:27, 11:31, 12:11; 1 Machabees 1:57.

[27] John 16:1-4.

[28] 1 Corinthians 11:27-9.

[29] Annibale Bugnini *The Reform of the Liturgy 1948-1975* (The Liturgical Press, 1990) p307 n6.

[30] Pius Parsch *The Church's Year of Grace* Vol. I p244.

[31] Congregation for Divine Worship, Instruction *Memoriale Domini* (1969). There are internal quotations and references to St Augustine, St Justin Martyr, the Congregation for Rites, and St Cyril of Jerusalem.

[32] Pope Benedict XVI *Light of the World: a Conversation with Peter Seewald* (Ignatius Press, 2010) pp158-59.

[33] St Thomas Aquinas *Summa Theologiae*, IIIa Q82 a3 c, quoted by the Office for the Liturgical Celebrations of the Supreme Pontiff: *Communion received on the tongue while kneeling* (2010).

[34] St Cyril of Jerusalem, *Mystagogical Catechesis* 5, 21f. The communicant is to cup his hands, left hand over right hand, and raise his hands to his mouth, with the Host in them.

[35] It was received either by intinction or by using a metal straw, called a fistula.

[36] 1 Corinthians 11:16.

[37] Congregation for the Doctrine of the Faith, Instruction *Inter Insigniores* (1976).

[38] Orthodox Jewish men, in liturgical prayer, use a double head-covering: the prayer-shawl (shallit) over the skull-cap (yarmulke).

[39] Pope John Paul II Apostolic Letter *Mulieris Dignitatem* (1988) 20.

[40] Pope John Paul II Post-Synodal Apostolic Exhortation *Vita Consecrata* (1996) 34.

[41] Manfred Hauke *Women in the Priesthood? A Systematic Analysis in the Light of the Order of Creation and Redemption* (Ignatius Press, 1986) p322 and p324.

[42] Pope John Paul II, Address to the Bishops of the North Western region of the United States, in their *ad limina* visit in 1998.

[43] Pontifical Commission *Ecclesia Dei*, Instruction Ecclesia Dei (2010) 24, 28. The issue is dealt with in *De Defectibus* X, which is contained in the 1962 *Missale Romanum*.

[44] *Notitiae* 30 (1994) 333-335.

[45] Christoph, Cardinal Schönborn *Loving the Church* (Ignatius Press, 1996) p205.

[46] *Sacrosanctum Concilium* 23.

[47] St Clement of Rome, *Ad Corinth.* (written c59-61).

[48] Quoted in Alcuin Reid *The Organic Development of the Liturgy* (Ignatius Press, 2005) pp20f.

[49] Today the Paxbrede is still used for the congregation in Spain and its former dominions, in the Extraordinary Form, and for the clergy in some religious orders, notably in the traditional Dominican Rite.

[50] Council of Trent, Session 22, Chapter V (1562).

[51] *Sacrosanctum Concilium* 91 and 93.

[52] Pope Pius V, Bull *Quo Primum* 1570.

[53] Anibale Bugnini *op. cit.* p300.

[54] Congregation for Divine Worship, Instruction *Quattuor Abhinc Annos* (1984).

[55] Pope John Paul II, Apostolic Letter given motu proprio, *Ecclesia Dei Adflicta* (1988).

[56] *Ibid*.

[57] Joseph Ratzinger *God and the World* (Ignatius Press, 2002) p416. (The German original was published in 2000.)

[58] Interestingly, many young people attached to the Extraordinary Form had attended World Youth Day in Cologne two years earlier, under the banner of the group 'Juventutem'.

[59] Bugnini *op. cit.* p297.

[60] Joseph, Cardinal Ratzinger, Lecture at Fontgombault, 2001.

[61] *A Bitter Trial: Evelyn Waugh and John Carmel Heenen on the Liturgical Changes* ed. Scott Reid (St Austin Press, 1996).

[62] See Fr Bryan Houghton *Judith's Marriage* (Credo House, 1987) p7.

[63] *Sacrosanctum Concilium* 37.

[64] *Unitatis Redintegratio* 17.

[65] Letter to Bishops accompanying *Summorum Pontificum*.

[66] Stratford Caldecott *Understanding the New Age* (Catholic Truth Society: 2006) p51.

[67] *Summorum Pontificum* Art. 9 section 1.

[68] This is sometimes also included in the Ordinary Form ritual, for example in the United States of America.

[69] *Summorum Pontificum* Art. 9 section 2; *cf. Universae Ecclesiae* 32.

[70] *1983 Code of Canon Law* 1174 § 2.

[71] Pope Paul VI Apostolic Letter *Sacrificium Laudis*.

[72] *Sacrosanctum Concilium* 84.

[73] Eamon Duffy *The Stripping of the Altars: Traditional Religion in England 1400-1580* (Yale University Press, 1994) p210.

[74] Published by Baronius Press, Angelus Press, and Carmel Books.

[75] Notably the *Small Ritual*, the standard book used in English parishes before Vatican II, and the *Parish Ritual*, the American equivalent which has recently been reprinted.

[76] Wine is blessed on the feast of St John (27th December), herbs on the Assumption, lilies on the feast of St Anthony of Padua (13th June), there is a special blessing of water on Epiphany, and so on.

[77] Congregation for Divine Worship, *Directory of Popular Piety and the Liturgy* (2001) 1.

[78] *Ibid.* 1; *cf. Sacrosanctum Concilium* 13.

[79] Letter to Bishops accompanying *Summorum Pontificum*.

[80] The parish of SS Gregory & Augustine, in Oxford, where sung Extraordinary Form Masses are celebrated regularly.

[81] www.miamiarch.org/CatholicDiocese.php?p=Article_13723162813374 Accessed 29/09/19.